What is Happening in our Primary Schools?

Henry Pluckrose

Basil Blackwell

First published 1987

© Henry Pluckrose 1987

Published by Basil Blackwell Ltd
108 Cowley Road
Oxford OX4 1JF
England

British Library Cataloguing in Publication Data
Pluckrose, Henry
    What is happening in our primary schools?
    1. Education, Elementary—Great Britain
    I. Title
    372.941   LA633
    ISBN 0–631–15907–X
    ISBN 0–631–15535–X Pbk

Typeset in 11/13pt Plantin
by Cambrian Typesetters, Frimley
Printed and bound in Great Britain
by Billings & Sons Limited, Worcester.

Contents

Acknowledgements

I would like to record my thanks to the people who have helped me in the preparation of this book: *James Nash* of Basil Blackwell for his helpful advice. *Hilary Devonshire* currently attached to The Urban Studies Centre, Poplar, London E14 for her perceptive comments and suggestions. *Roz Sullivan* for her careful preparation of the typescript. The Editor of *The Sunday Times* for permission to quote the extract from an article by Adam Hopkins (published in October 1975) (page 26) and to the Education Officer, ILEA for permission to quote from an unpublished report (page 67).

Introduction

On Wednesday I was an 18-year-old schoolboy, on Thursday an enlisted soldier. This sudden transition from adolescence to manhood was not of my choice. Conscription had touched me – as it did the generations before me and the one which was to follow.

Coming as I did from a working class family, I did not find my new colleagues (mainly lads from the Rhondda) too frightening. What did surprise me was how little they knew about the things I had long taken for granted – things like books and the topics discussed in 'serious' newspapers and magazines. What also surprised me was how much more than me they knew about life and how ignorant I was of its richness and variety. The seven years I had spent in a second-rate London grammar school had given me a superficial cultural gloss. But the school, the image of the world it projected and the demands it made upon me were quite unrelated to the reality of life beyond its gates.

The Ministry of Defence must have been aware that I – and many another like me – were unsuitable material for turning into real soldiers. I quickly found myself removed from the infantry and transferred to a corps which had originally been established to help semi-illiterate recruits towards literacy and numeracy. By the age of 19, after a very short period of training, I was posted to an education centre. Six months after leaving school I had become a school master!

Few of my pupils were young recruits. One man, well over

40 years of age, sticks in my mind. He came to me late in the evening, a letter in his hand. 'It's from my wife. Can you please read it to me?'

I scanned the pages. The message was frank and brutal. Paraphrased, it said: 'Stay away. I have another man. I need you no more'. As gently as I could I conveyed the drift of the letter (if not its tone). With tears running down his face he thanked me, remarking as he left 'If I could have read this myself I could have had my pain in private'.

'If I could have read this . . .'

A similar episode was to occur a few years later. In 1954, fresh from teacher training, I was coping with my very first class of eight year olds in a primary school in a deprived area of South London.

Peter's father came in to see me. Having been advised by my headteacher that Mr T was a person to avoid, I retreated behind my desk for safety. He strode across the room, seized my hand and proceeded to shake it fiercely. Then in broad Cockney he explained why he had come.

'You see I can't read. My wife can't read. My mother can't read. Her mother can't read. My (son) John can't read, neither can Marie, Ciss, Chris or Harry. But somehow you've taught Pete. Thank you. Now we can find out what's coming on tele before the announcer tells us.'

With that he left. Pete looked triumphant. I felt drained . . . never before had Pete's father visited school and left without bloodshed.

When speaking or writing about teaching I often recall these two incidents. They serve to remind me of my central task. As a teacher I must try to provide all the children in my care with a range of skills. To cope with everyday life many varied skills will be needed and of these skills none are more important than mastery of the spoken and written word.

Another thought often occurs. There is a view, widely held, that there was once a Golden Educational Age when every child could read at seven and only those retarded by accident of birth were unable to recite their tables and compute.

In the army I taught many men like Pete's dad. As a teacher I have received many letters and notes, ill-constructed and poorly penned, which suggest that his problem is not that uncommon. Adequate mastery of the written word is something which schools have failed to give to far too many. For some this will provide a life-long handicap; for others, adult literacy programmes may go some way to making good the damage.

This book is neither a cry for a return to an age which has passed or a plea for a new, more radical, approach to the education of young children. It should be seen as a critical, albeit personal, analysis of the tensions and problems which will need to be resolved if our primary schools are to meet the hopes of the parents who use them, the aspirations of the teachers who work in them, the plans of the local authorities who administer them and the dreams of the politicians who watch over them. Alongside these groups is another, even more important than any of those listed.

It is a group with no power and no voice. It is the consumer group we call children.

Henry Pluckrose

1 What do children need of school?

Having been a teacher for over 30 years it might seem strange that I should begin a book on primary education by reflecting on the significance of schooling.

And yet I must. Compulsory state education for all is, in the historical sense, a recent phenomenon. In most European countries the move towards education for all dates from the nineteenth century. The English and Welsh, who look back on the year 1870 (Forster's Education Act) as the effective starting point of a state system, were not the first in Europe to realise that a literate workforce would be needed to meet the ever more complex demands of industry.

Provision of elementary schooling was a reflection of economic need. A pool of people who could read and keep ledgers was essential if the world of commerce were to expand. Expenditure on education was not regarded (except perhaps by 'woolly intellectuals') as a means of giving opportunity to the masses. It made economic sense. Liberal education for those who could afford to pay for it was unlikely to be required by the son of a bootmaker in Northampton, or for his daughter who was destined to spend her days 'in service'.

A further reason for this interest in education has been suggested. The Victorian period was one of tremendous economic and social change. The old values which had underpinned Britain when it was an agrarian society were threatened by a new urban poor. The squire and the rector, and the traditions which they represented, had no power or influence in the squalid housing estates which grew up round each new factory and mill. To many it seemed clear that if liberal capitalism (of the sort advocated by Disraeli) were not to be swept away by revolution, the largely illiterate workforce must be encouraged to believe that their welfare would be protected by the new rulers – the powerful middle class. This goal could be realised through making education more widely available. State education was not simply the natural conse-quence of giving votes to the masses, or a belief in the need, as one Minister put it, to 'educate our masters'. Education was also seen as the 'sovereign remedy for all ills', a means by which the tears in the cloth of society could be cobbled together and its divisions patched.

Over a hundred years have passed since Forster's Act. Go into our primary schools and superficially there are great differences between the environment which we provide now and that which was provided in the 1890s. Today's bright and open classrooms with their informal furniture seem light years away from the first school in which I taught. As recently as thirty years ago my basic equipment consisted of iron desks with attached iron seats (the whole unit bolted to the floor to discourage movement) a blackboard and a teacher's desk. Sets of books, refillable inkwells, steel nibs, chalk, exercise paper (ruled and margined) and the occasional visual aid (a world map) were the tools of teaching.

Like many another teacher of my generation I stood, talked and thereby – I hoped – taught. The children sat, listened and accidentally learned. The impact of my teaching was probably immensely forgettable. Yet I was fulfilling my task – the filling of young minds with facts.

Today we look to our primary schools to make learning rather more adventurous than this. We have come to expect that the programmes undertaken will fit the child, matching his or her age, aptitude and ability with a learning experience which will be challenging, satisfying, invigorating and self-rewarding. We have moved away from daily table chanting and spelling tests, when the mastery of English involved little more than fitting appropriate words into gaps in simple sentences, when reading was learned parrot fashion from a primer.

And yet *have* things changed so radically? We may have moved on from the steel nib and the blackboard, but are we not educating our children for much the same reasons as we were 50 years ago? The changes we see in our classrooms have been in style rather than in objectives.

Some years ago *The Sunday Times* invited parents (representing a wide range of social backgrounds) to list the things which they felt to be significant for their children in their years of primary schooling. Many readers expressed surprise at the findings, but I was not among them. Topping the list of priorities was 'happiness'. Much lower down were the traditional school subjects of reading, writing and computation.

Indeed parents' perceptions of school often differ from those of academics and politicians. Reflecting upon the findings of a survey of 1000 Scottish parents (published in the Spring of 1987), Michael Adler of Edinburgh University observed 'Parents choose schools on the basis of vague impressions. Government ministers seem to think that they look at a pile of brochures. Most parents do not assess what a school has to offer.' His research confirmed this view. At primary school level the great majority of the 400 parents interviewed were more concerned with the school's distance from home and how rough the children were than with class size and educational standards.

In my time as headteacher of a primary school, similar observations were often made to me. After being taken round by a six or seven year old, parents visiting the school for the first time were given the opportunity to talk to me or to one of my colleagues. The discussions rarely centred upon how quickly John or Sandra might master mathematics or reading. These elements of the school programme would, it was assumed, somehow 'come'. What was demanded of me, however, was that school would provide a secure, happy environment in which children would have an opportunity to share ideas, to develop their social skills and to discover their particular individual gifts.

All of which, I would argue, sounds impossibly idealistic. But is it? Of course the primary years mark a time when children must master language. They need to be shown how to shape and extend the language of home, street, playgroup and nursery. Yet all too often the gulf between the words of everyday life and the words found in graded reader and story book prevents an easy transition from speech to written language.

In my books and lectures I have repeatedly emphasised the importance of talk. Children must be given the opportunity to talk through their ideas before they are expected to write them down. Indeed, it is vital to encourage talk after every new experience – whether that experience is obtained through reading a book, meeting an expert (eg a museum curator) or making a visit to a castle, a factory or a farm.

The place of talk is equally important in children's introduction to mathematics. Children's talk indicates to the gifted teacher the intellectual and perceptual level which each child has reached. Some would argue that mathematics is not about talk – it's about calculations, fractions, decimal points, four rules and many different sorts of measure! I think not.

Children come to school at the age of five already enriched with a whole range of mathematical experiences. They do not come to school as empty vessels. They will have experienced distance ('It was a long way to the seaside'); time ('Please can I stay up longer?'); quantity ('Can I have some more sweets?'); capacity ('My glass is empty') and comparison ('I'm taller than John'). They will have sorted bricks and arranged them in neat piles (sorting and setting). They will probably have learned to count. Many will have played with constructional toys through which, unknowingly, they will have gained some insight into the fundamentals of shape.

These examples may seem to be somewhat removed from the experience of a child who has grown up in an inner-city slum. Yet the toddler playing in a scruffy backstreet is, in the process, drinking in and assimilating experiences which can be drawn upon by school. The language may be non-traditional, the experiences different. Every child new to the reception class has pre-school experience upon which the teacher can build.

Experience is taken by the perceptive teacher and used as the starting point for further discovery. The fact that an infant child can complete correctly such sums as $9 + 3 = 12$ and work through page upon page of identical problems is no indication that that child's understanding of mathematics (or number) is being deepened. Learning by rote is no guarantee that learning has been achieved. True learning implies understanding. How many of my readers can give the answer to $3/8 \div 15/16$ but are unable to explain why the answer is $2/5$?[1]

Modern approaches to the teaching of mathematics have centred upon the child's perception of his or her world. Advocates of this kind of approach take everyday experiences (like cooking) and use them to clarify those words which we use to explain mathematics and to vivify the abstractions which are central to the subject. Learning is therefore seen in terms of where the child *is* rather than where we hope he might be.

In both of these key areas – language and mathematics – the effective school takes those things which the children have subconsciously learned in their own private and personal world and builds upon them. By listening to her children's language (which, to quote T S Eliot, 'is the fluid in which all else is suspended') the teacher is able to go some way in interpreting their individual levels of development and maturation. Her programme will aim at extending and deepening understanding. To do this she must begin her teaching from the point which the children have reached.

Language stems from experience. If we do nothing we will have little to talk about. If our minds are not actively engaged and challenged by the world in which we live, we may well slip inexorably into the world of day-dream and make-believe.

I have consistently argued that the primary school should provide children with an ever widening range of experience. It should provide a place where children can meet and talk with adults who live in and serve the local community – the fireman, the nurse, the secretary, the shopkeeper, the police officer, the craftsman and craftswoman. Through exposure to the rich variety of skills, attitudes, gifts, life- and workstyles found in ordinary people, children can be shown that all individuals are unique and that it is their differences (rather than their similarities) which are of value to society.

Children also need help to move out from the parochialism of their world. The urban street and the rural village are both, in their different ways, educational backwaters. The village child needs to be aware of the noise and movement of the big city. The urban child needs to be given opportunity to explore the quieter reflective world of woodland and meadow. Both need the opportunity to explore beach and castle, to look in on a busy workshop, to wander round a ruin, to wonder at a megalithic monument, to gaze at strange animals in a wildlife park. Both also need to be helped to understand the nature of the changes occurring in the area in which they live – whether disappearing hedgerows or the closing down of a street market.

Such experiences vivify learning and give children the opportunity to talk and, through talk, to explore ideas. They also encourage children to question, providing a *real* reason to turn to books and tapes and material stored on floppy disk.

All young children (and many older ones too) have this need to *do* and to explore the world through their senses. The senses provide the means through which they drink in experience and personalise it. Learning through first-hand experience provides the framework into which information obtained in other ways (from books, television and radio) can be fitted.

This developing and deepening exploration of the world through a marriage of language and the senses is not all the primary years should provide. It is also of great importance that children should be given opportunity to develop their skills. It is of little value to a child if he or she can express him or herself in words but is unable to write in a legible hand. It is pointless to invite children to question if they are never challenged to test, and so justify, their initial findings. To be able to hypothesise is important, to be able to evaluate findings is vital.

It is for this reason, perhaps, that there has been a move, clearly indicated in the curriculum guidelines recently produced by HM Inspectorate,[2] to emphasise the importance of skills-based learning. An approach to education through the mastery of thinking skills will, it is hoped, help establish questions appropriate to particular subject disciplines. 'How do we test our ideas?' is a question which we could ask about an experiment with seeds, struggling to grow while deprived of adequate light. It is also a question we would ask about the tomb of a knight, whose collar suggests he might have been a Lancastrian. The method we adopt to arrive at an answer will be peculiar to the enquiry (or discipline) we are exploring.

Linked with a curriculum which centres upon practical enquiry, is the need to develop in children appropriate methods of presenting ideas. Some findings are best presented in paint, for others, poetry or prose may be more suitable; some can be presented through models, others in the form of graphs and charts. Children quickly realise that there is no one approach which can be universally followed. Mathematics can be explained through the written word 'We went to the main road at 10.00 am to begin our traffic count. We did it like this . . .' These findings would probably be presented in tabular form linked to a graph and a scale map to show the exact position where the count was taken.

Young children tend – almost by accident – to integrate academic disciplines, to interpret the world in comprehensible 'wholes'. To paraphrase Mr Polly, it's only school that turns the young child from someone who wonders at the marvels around him or her into someone who sees them only in terms of history and geography.

Doing, experiencing, discussing, taking part, sharing . . .

the hopeful parent would surely welcome schooldays for their children based upon a programme in which these elements enjoy a central part.

To these must be added one further ingredient, the arts. Civilisation has developed because men and women have continually struggled to master their environment. Wood, clay, metals, fibres, earth, bone, stone, skin have been fashioned into the fabric of everyday life. All that we use in our modern world is a comment upon the delicate balance of human hand, eye and brain. This harmony of hand and eye and the immersion of the child in crafts which are almost as old as humankind itself, should be central to the work of every school. A child who has been stretched emotionally and imaginatively in fashioning a pot from a lump of clay or weaving upon a simple loom will come, through the process of doing, to learn much about himself and gain some understanding of the pain, pleasure and struggle which underpin craftsmanship. To follow the process from clay lump to glazed decoration demands discipline.

Norman, an aggressive nine year old, exploded at a boy walking in front of him who had thoughtlessly trodden on a painting which had fallen onto the floor. 'I don't like her much', he said, pointing to its creator 'but you don't tread on it. You know how hard it is to paint like that'. This little episode shows how Norman regarded the stress which accompanies any art form when it has been seriously undertaken.

For me the arts embrace far more than the visual and dimensional. Early childhood is also a time when drama, dance and music have a significant part to pay. The mastery of a musical instrument, the ability to interpret notes, a feeling for rhythm, the disciplining of the body through formal physical education and informal dance are all central to a child's needs in the transition from babyhood through adolescence to maturity.

Underpinning all that I have written is an assumption . . . that the education process must be based upon the child. This assumption is far from fashionable. It makes demands upon us, the adults. It challenges our neat theories. It invites continual reassessment of our role, our place in school, of the real significance of all those elements which we (as adults) feel *ought* to have a place in the school programme.

The cynic might be excused for observing that although these ideals should be met, they are impossible to realise. Teachers are expensive to employ. Is it possible to organise state schools on the basis of a curriculum which is built around the age, aptitude and abilities of individual children? Can society afford the luxury of providing young children with the beginnings of a liberal education?

To this there can be but one response. Our schools have been failing. They have failed because of the tyranny which stems from a narrow curriculum rather than because the curriculum has been too broad or too diffuse. The reports made by members of Her Majesty's Inspectorate have, over the past eighteen months, regularly drawn attention to the failure of teachers to pitch their expectations high enough. Children, the reports emphasise, *can* achieve, *can* create, *can* be responsible. A dreary diet of lessons based upon textbook and worksheet is never going to inspire children to regard schooling with enthusiasm, nor will it provide the base on which a personal commitment to learning can be built.

Critics of a more open approach to young children's learning often cite the Plowden Report (1966) as the source and inspiration of all that has been wrong with our primary schools. 'It encouraged work that was not sufficiently rigorous.' 'It put the child at the centre of things.' 'It encouraged permissiveness.'

The view that a child-centred approach suddenly swept across England in the 1960s and 1970s is quite inaccurate. In some areas – like Oxfordshire, the West Riding of Yorkshire, Bristol and Berkshire – there was change. In many other parts of the country, primary schools followed a curriculum in which formal activities in number and language occupied the bulk of children's time in school. Had the Plowden Report

received more support from politicians, academics and educationalists and had its recommendations been applied rather
more vigorously across the country,[3] I think our primary
schools would today be much less open to criticism.

The response to parental discontent and pupil underachieve-
ment has been to try to design curriculum guidelines. Some
authorities have issued broad discussion documents; others
have been rather more prescriptive (in Croydon, for example,
parents have been given a checklist of skills against which to
evaluate their children. From it I learn that a seven year old
has achieved a satisfactory standard if he can tell the time
accurately in units of five minutes!). The reason for guidelines
is not hard to find. Education has become too important an
issue to leave to teachers. If teachers are failing, then basic
curriculum decisions must be taken from teaching staff.

The move towards a more centralised curriculum began in
the late 1970s after the abortive 'Great Debate on Education'
(See Chapter 2). The 1980s have been marked by an avalanche
of documents from both local and central government. Each
document seeks to lay down a curriculum policy, define a
subject area and stress the need for an education programme
which is 'coherent and continuous'.

Not all of these initiatives have centred on basic curriculum
areas (like English or mathematics). Local authorities whose
members believe that their particular ideologies should be
furthered through schools have added their own ingredients.
The directives are unequivocal. Every school must have a
multi-ethnic policy . . . Every child must be made aware of
the danger of sexual stereotyping . . . No teacher will wear or
display on his person or car a badge which indicates support
for a pressure group (like CND or Greenpeace).

All of these guidelines, many of them well-intentioned and
prepared with care, have been aimed at making primary
schools fulfil a predetermined function – to prepare young
children for the secondary stage and to give them enthusiasm
for learning. They are doomed to fail.

In many European countries a similar method of 'criteria

targeting' has been applied to schools. At seven, the child will learn this; at eight the child will learn that; by nine years of age this information will be assimilated . . . but we must not teach this, or this, or this.

Such a system would be appropriate if human beings were made like cars on an automated production line. A unit of mathematics at one point is followed by a unit of language or history at another, the whole being completed after eleven years with a final coat of educational gloss. Fortunately, human beings do not learn in this way. The charge I have often heard when working overseas that 'school is boring' is a comment on the quality of life in the classroom. The poet, Laurie Lee, describes his schooldays with critical detachment: but they were boring for him too. 'School', he writes, seemed to have one aim, 'to keep us out of the air and from following the normal pursuits of the fields . . . Crabby's science of dates and sums and writing seemed a typical invention of her own . . . prison labour like picking oakum or sewing sacks.'[4]

The boredom and disenchantment which can follow upon criteria targeting produce one significant side effect. In order to standardise children's learning, teachers tend to standardise their approach to teaching. As I know from personal experience one Bulgarian or Yugoslavian school is very much like its neighbour. The books are identical for each group, and children follow the same activities. The teachers (trapped between book and prescribed purpose) follow a pattern. They too become mechanistic.

Mechanistic methods, once developed, are difficult to break. In Sweden (a country I have visited regularly since 1976) there is a desire, expressed by both teachers and senior government educational advisors, to use the most recent läroplan (the centrally imposed school curriculum) as a starting point for creative teaching which takes into account the needs of children and the way in which they learn. The desire is rarely reflected in classroom practice.

The intention, to create a curriculum which gives equal opportunity to all, is admirable. The long term consequence is far less satisfying. Teachers are trained to teach to a plan. Children are expected to conform to a plan. Constrained by such a straight-jacket, personal growth (of teacher or taught) becomes virtually impossible.

Yet the debate is still open. There are some (politicians and academics) who believe that it is essential to give a more formal framework to our primary schools. There are others (amongst whom I am one) who would argue that we need to give young children the opportunity to develop fully at their own pace and in their own individual ways.

Several other elements add to the stress which these tensions bring into our schools. Technological change affects all of us. The computer in the classroom and the television and video in the sitting room are symbols of this change. We cannot (either at school or at home) isolate children from the impact that technology has made upon our everyday lives.

Technological change brings in its wake social change. The modern nuclear family may reflect the mobility which technology has brought. But it has made emotional and social demands upon family life which parents and children are all-too-often ill-equipped to bear.

The society in which our children live and grow is characterised by contrasting and conflicting values. Materialism brings in its wake as many problems as it does blessings. We have improved the standard of living but in the process forgotten how to live. We appear to value the things which education can bring but are in danger of losing, through an ever-tightening grip on schools, the value and respect we should show to each child.

Notes and references

1 The mechanical method is simple to master:
$$3/8 \div 15/16 = 3/8 \times 16/15 = 2/5$$
It is much more difficult to explain the second stage (the inversion of the fraction following the division sign and the substitution of the $\div$ by $\times$).

2 From 1984–85 a range of discussion papers on the curriculum appropriate to 5–16 year olds was prepared by the DES (HMSO Publications). See Appendix, page 158, for details.
3 In 1978 it was estimated that only 6% of primary schools in England and Wales followed a Plowden-type programme.
4 From *Cider with Rosie* by Laurie Lee (Penguin Books, 1962) – Crabby was his teacher.

2 The post-war years

Writing this book has encouraged me to reflect upon the changes which have occurred in primary education in England and Wales since the end of World War II. Looking back I can now see that some of the happenings through which I lived professionally were destined to be profound and far reaching in their impact and to become milestones of educational change.

Some were significant when they happened: it was easy to grasp that the changes they foreshadowed would be fundamental. Yet to give instant opinions on the long term impact of the many educational reports, speeches, Parliamentary debates, learned researches, books, ideas and happenings which marked the years through which I worked as a teacher was quite impossible. Looking back into the past from the security of the present it is possible to pinpoint those elements which led to a change of viewpoint, the emergence of a new approach or a hasty retreat into well tried ways. When they happened, however, I was usually unable to foresee or judge their future significance.

Before I attempt to describe in detail the principal strands which have created the contemporary primary school it is necessary to appreciate the difficulty of isolating and then evaluating the contribution made by each of them. Let me illustrate the difficulty with three simple examples.

The educational debate during the years immediately following the war concentrated more upon the nature of secondary schooling than it did upon the primary stage. Should secondary schools be reorganised, and the long-established grammar schools (to which entry was gained by selection at 11) be abolished and replaced by comprehensives? Although the Labour Party adopted a policy of 'comprehensive education for all' in 1951 no political action to implement it was taken for another 14 years.

In 1965 Anthony Crossland, the Labour Secretary of State for Education, issued Circular 10/65 which requested those local authorities which had not already done so to submit to him their proposals for the reorganisation of their secondary schools along comprehensive lines. The circular pushed local authorities towards change. Although not all authorities responded (and it was those with strong Conservative majorities which failed to do so), the effect of the circular was dramatic. The ideal of providing an adequate and satisfying secondary education for all (and not just for the few who were fortunate enough to be able to pass a selection test at 11) seemed close to realisation.

The implementation of comprehensive education was not just significant for teachers in secondary schools, who were forced to reassess their curriculum and school organisation. Its effect on primary schools was equally far reaching. Long before the appearance of Circular 10/65 a small number of primary school teachers had argued that secondary school selection should not determine the primary school curriculum. But in practice, for the great majority of schools, the selection procedure acted as a straightjacket. Primary schools tended to be judged, by parents and teachers, on the number of grammar school places (or 'scholarships') won each year. In many cases, therefore, the programme followed by primary schools was determined by the need to prepare a minority of pupils for an examination at 11. From the age of seven, weekly, termly and yearly testing in the '3Rs' provided a yardstick against which each child was measured.[1] If successful a place in the 'A' stream was guaranteed and beyond it lay grammar school and perhaps college or university. The 'diet' followed by the 'A' stream children was invariably tied to the type of test which the local authority or the local selective schools set. It was invariably mechanistic and, providing the brighter children in each 'A' stream were adequately 'drilled', success was assured. And the slower learners? For these the primary schools provided a gentle haven before they transferred to the local secondary modern school. The selection test merely served to confirm something which they already knew – in the academic race they were already failures.

The removal of selection at 11 gave primary school teachers the opportunity to relate their work to the needs of all the children and to make the school day meaningful for each individual in their care. No longer (as happened in the primary school in which I first worked) would the teacher responsible for the fourth year 'scholarship' class leave them as soon as the examination day (in January) was passed – going to prepare the third year 'A' stream for next year's examinations with a diet of chanted tables, spelling tests, drills in mental arithmetic, weekly essays, grammatical analysis, punctuation, and worksheets based on past intelligence test papers.[2] For many 'A' stream children there was little place on the timetable for music, dance, art, craft, poetry, the humanities – subjects which were dismissed as window-dressing by some of my professional colleagues.

When in 1986 Kenneth Baker, Secretary of State for Education and Science in Margaret Thatcher's second administration introduced the idea of City Technology Colleges for children from the age of 11, the spectre of selection reappeared. How might this affect, I wonder, the programme which children follow in the primary schools in the area which they serve?

Our primary schools have also been shaped, influenced and changed in a conscious way through Act of Parliament. It should be realised, however, that the changes which flow from these Acts are not always those which were originally conceived. When the Warnock Committee suggested in its report (1978) that every effort should be made to assimilate the handicapped, whenever appropriate, into mainstream schools, it was apparent that implementing this would mark a fundamental change in education provision. The Act which followed the report (1981) was seen by parents, by teachers and by members of the caring professions as marking the beginning of a new, radical approach to the way in which society responded to the needs of the handicapped child.

As a headteacher of a state primary school I was immediately aware that I would be asking the staff who worked with me to take on new responsibilities. The handicapped children who joined school forced us to look again at the provision we made for children. The fact that the school building was not adapted for wheelchairs; that toilets were too narrow for the chair-bound; that equipment was needed to dispose of soiled napkins, as well as special beds upon which children could be cleaned and changed; was noted by the local authority and quietly ignored.

This example serves to indicate how comparatively easy it is to legislate for change and how difficult it can be to implement the legislation. But the problem transcends the lack of physical resources. Inadequate funding combined with inadequate staffing often means that the ideals which are central to a change of programme are rarely realised. It may eventually become apparent that the successful implementation of the 1981 Act was made impossible because in the early stages of its introduction too many teachers were frustrated at the lack of support they received.

Not all the milestones of change are as immediately obvious as a Government Circular, the report of a standing committee, or the passage of a Bill through Parliament. When the first parental rumblings voicing criticism of a hitherto unknown junior school in Islington, North London, became public, few watchers of the educational scene imagined that they marked the beginning of a long-running drama which would fill many column inches in the daily press as well as provide material for a TV documentary.

The conflict was not lacking in human interest. Young

children, it was alleged, were being given autonomy beyond their years. While children 'followed their own interests',[3] the teaching staff, strong on ideals but weak in their implementation of them, spent much time engaged in heated debate with parents and with each other.

Even when the conflict entered the public domain, the significance of what came to be described as 'The Scandal of Tyndale' was not at first apparent. Yet the report of the Enquiry (presided over by a QC) set up by the Inner London Education Authority to resolve the dispute had the effect of fuelling a campaign for educational retrenchment.

The fall-out from Tyndale remains. The failure of a small group of teachers (who even if they were not professionally inept were certainly politically naïve) was used to provide ammunition for an attack on schools whose approach to learning diverged from the traditional.

Unacceptable standards of behaviour and attainment at Tyndale did not mean that *all* schools following an enquiry or discovery approach to learning were similarly failing. Sadly, commentators and writers in the mass circulation dailies sometimes lack the ability to discriminate. As the story of a collapsing school filled the headlines of press, television and radio, many teachers responded by retreating from the more informal approaches to learning which non-selection at 11 had encouraged, into the safety of more traditional methods.

Within a few years the William Tyndale School returned to normal, and it is now a popular and flourishing institution. But its collapse had served to focus attention upon many of the tensions within the school system. Who runs schools? teachers, local educational authorities, or central government (who indirectly provide much of the resources)? Had Tyndale collapsed because its teachers had no understanding of the expectations of the parent body? Should parents have a right to determine how schools were run? Should parents (who have only experienced education as consumers) be allowed to shape the schooldays of their children? Might not trained teachers be expected to know what is best?

The debate prompted by Tyndale continues. When the teaching staff at the school developed their radical approaches to learning, they surely had no idea of the consequences of their action.

These three examples, juxtaposed, serve to highlight the nature of educational change. Acts of Parliament and committee recommendations do cause a shift of emphasis, but social and political pressures, academic research, and evolving classroom practice can be just as influential. Developments and changes in education must not be considered in isolation, unrelated to the political, economic and social climate of the times in which they emerge.

Since this book is concerned with developments in the education of young children since the 1950s, the most appropriate starting point is the 1944 (Butler) Education Act. Section I of this Act clearly sets out how education is to be administered and identifies the bodies which are to be responsible for the implementation of educational policies.

> It shall be lawful for his Majesty to appoint a Minister whose duty it shall be to promote the education of the people of England and Wales and the progressive development of institutions devoted to that purpose and to secure the effective execution by the local authorities, under his control and direction, of the national policy for providing a varied and comprehensive educational service in every area.
>
> *(Education Act* 1944. Part I)

Thus the Minister (Secretary of State) is responsible to Parliament for local educational administration. In effect his powers are somewhat circumscribed by both tradition and the organisational pattern of local government which developed in England and Wales following upon the Education Act of 1870 and the reshaping of local government in 1888.

The apparent abdication of power by central government is illustrated by two examples taken from the turn of the century. In 1898 the rigidly enforced 'code' of practice which laid down curriculum guidelines for elementary schools (Standard 1 to 7) was abolished. Seven years later in 1905, the Board of Education published its *Handbook of Suggestions for the consideration of Teachers in Elementary Schools.* It included in its preface the following statement:

> The only uniformity of practice that the Board of Education desires to see in the teaching of Public Elementary schools is that each teacher should think for himself and work out for himself such methods of teaching as may use his powers to the best advantage and be best suited to the particular needs and conditions of the school. Uniformity in detail of practice is not desirable even if it were attainable. But freedom implies a corresponding responsibility in its use.

Although the centrally devised programme which all elementary schools then followed was not abolished until 1926, the freedom given to state school teachers to devise their own methodology to suit the school's particular needs was a radical innovation.

In effect, the 1944 Act confirmed the idea of partnership; that central government and local authorities would share responsibility for the running of the nation's schools. Supporting this was a further partnership, that which had been established almost informally between each teaching force and the local authority for whom they worked. Headteachers and their staffs ran schools for the authority. In all major areas (secondary school selection, the applications of financial grants to specific activities, school building, staffing levels . . .) the local authority made decisions and the teaching force were the agents through which policy was implemented.

Beyond this, however, teachers were given considerable autonomy. The way individual schools were organised, the pattern of the school day, the drafting and implementation of the curriculum remained, and continues to remain, the responsibility of the staff of each school. Of course schools were (and are) inspected both by inspectors from the local authority and by members of Her Majesty's Inspectorate for Schools. These visitations, which might be formal or informal, seek to establish whether the school is following a programme appropriate to the needs, ages and abilities of the pupils who attend it.

The degree of freedom which teachers in England are allowed to exercise and the responsibility with which they exercise the power vested in them is a major factor in the unique nature of English primary education. It could be argued that the long-running teachers' dispute of 1984–87 has eroded and undermined this trust. If teachers cannot be trusted to organise schools in the interests of their pupils, should not the state restrict their autonomy? The dispute – coming as it did in the aftermath of Tyndale – served to confirm the view that the teaching force was too independent. Although, as we have seen, there has been no core curriculum[4] since 1905, teachers have based their work upon key elements – that young children should be helped towards the mastery of the written and spoken word, and to have sufficient understanding of number.

The freedom to experiment, to organise classrooms in a way which supported and encouraged children's learning, and which incidentally (though not haphazardly) covered the key areas of the curriculum led to many innovations. Influential Inspectors like Christian Schiller of the Department of Education and Science; headteachers like Tom Johns in Oxfordshire; classroom teachers like Sybil Marshall; lecturers in colleges of education, like Len Marsh; directors of education like Alec Clegg in the West Riding of Yorkshire; and creative thinkers like Robin Tanner, Edith Moorhouse and John Coe; used the opportunity which the massive restructuring of state education gave and were instrumental in building up, for the first time, a coherent philosophy for the English primary school.

The movement was not organised, it grew and flourished in individual schools and in individual classrooms. In these schools and classrooms the more traditional approaches to teaching and learning were rejected, not because they were traditional but because their teachers came to realise that through a programme of learning which was based upon the qualities and gifts of each child, higher standards could be achieved. 'Standards' in this context applies not just to reading, writing and arithmetic but to important intangibles like self-confidence, responsibility and self-discipline.

It was against such a background of innovation that the Plowden Committee began its enquiry into the state of primary schools in England and Wales. The Committee, which began its work in August 1963 and reported in November 1966, visited primary schools across England and Wales as well as in Denmark, Sweden, France, Poland, the USA and the USSR.

As an analysis of the nature of the child in the primary years and of the way children learn, the Plowden Report ranks as the most detailed study of the early years of schooling ever produced. The schools which would have resulted had its recommendations been fully implemented would have been noticeably different from those found in most other developed nations. Throughout the Plowden Report runs the assumption that what is taught in schools (ie what we, the adults expect children to learn) must relate to where the child is (intellectually, social, emotionally) rather than to where we think the child ought to be. This premise is in direct opposition to the view, currently fashionable, that defined and prescribed academic targets should be set for each stage of a child's progress through school.[5]

The philosophy which Plowden embraced rejected this thesis because the evidence upon which it drew (demonstrated in the quality of learning in the schools which it visited) ran counter to this belief. Being human, children do not respond to learning targets imposed arbitrarily by outside agencies (be the agency a ministry of education, a university professor or a well-meaning politician). Criteria targeting (ie working towards a predetermined objective) is appropriate to the robots on a car production line: it is quite inappropriate to the education of children. This problem faced by the teacher who sees himself as deliverer of prepacked information is admirably expressed by Caldwell Cook, who worked in the Perse School, Cambridge. In *The Playway* first published in 1917, he observed:

> The teacher works, whether consciously or unconsciously on his own lines and not in and for his children. The teacher may have a beautiful system, graded and ordered . . . and approved by His Majesty's Inspector. But what if the child's mind does not work orderly? What will His Majesty do then, poor thing?

In emphasising the place which the child played in his own learning process, Plowden was not covering new ground. Susan Isaacs, perhaps the most significant English educationalist of this century, stressed the same point in her book *The Children we Teach*.

> One is brought back to the fundamental conclusion that throughout the Primary years it is the children's activity that is the key to full development. The child's doing, the child's active social experience and his own thinking and talking are the chief means of his education . . . words cannot be substituted for things. Theoretical reasoning is a dead letter to the child unless it is closely anchored to practical issues.

Some of the recommendations of the Plowden Report were implemented with enthusiasm. It stressed, for example, the importance of cooperation between home and school.

> What matters most are the attitudes of teachers to parents and parents to teachers – whether there is genuine mutual respect, whether the parents understand what the schools are doing for individual children and (whether) teachers realise how dependent they are upon parental support.

There are now many more manifestations of this shared

responsibility. Today every school has members elected from the parent body on its Board of Governors.[6]

Others of its recommendations, such as an expansion of nursery education, transfer to secondary school at 12 (rather than 11) and to junior departments at 8 (instead of 7), were introduced in a piecemeal fashion. Some local education authorities reorganised their primary schools on the first and middle school pattern recommended by Plowden (eg Surrey, Isle of Wight, Suffolk), but the great majority continued to follow the established 5–7, 7–11 pattern. In recent years some local authorities which introduced first and middle schools following Plowden have reverted to this more traditional structure.

The significance of the Plowden Report lay not so much in its recommendations but in what it sought to proclaim. The primary curriculum was to be active rather than passive and one where every appropriate practical experience should be used to underpin theoretical learning.

The Report stressed the importance of taking children into the curriculum-making process. If children were *shown how* to learn rather than *told what* to learn, the skills and processes which apply to all subject areas were more likely to be mastered.

Having unequivocally given its support to child-centred learning, the Plowden Report also emphasised the responsibility which was entrusted to teachers by society. Teachers must always realise that the 'obvious purpose of school is to fit children to the society in which they will grow up'.

The Plowden Report had stressed that children 'were at the centre of the education process', but what did this mean? The main emphasis of the Report (its concentration upon a child-centred approach, and rather lightweight treatment of the teacher's role) provoked academic criticism. Professor Peters of the London Institute of Education, for example, centred his reservations upon the Report's implications. If the purpose of teaching is to expedite learning, then a person who is taught is likely to learn more effectively than one who is not.

'Educational half-truths' presented as 'panaceas' were, he argued, no substitute for 'properly thought out educational theory'.

Could one, Peters asked, expect children to learn in the somewhat haphazard fashion that unfettered child-centredness seemed to commend? His response was unequivocal. To learn effectively it is necessary to grasp certain principles and rules, and these rules would be particular to individual academic disciplines. For 'a child (needs) to grasp from the inside what following rules means and take rules into himself between which he has to choose'.

R F Dearden, a colleague of Peters at the London Institute, took a similar stance. The task of the teacher was to help children 'obtain insight into certain basic ways in which human experience has been developed and elaborated'. Thus the curriculum of the primary school, he suggested, should be seen as a beginning, where children are helped to develop an understanding of Mathematics, Science, History and the Arts alongside the mastery of the basics of their mother tongue.

The years following upon the Plowden Report were ones in which primary practice was subject to intense and continued re-evaluation. The child's 'instinctive' desire to learn (taken for granted by supporters of a child-centred approach) was questioned and subjected to the academic scrutiny which the authors of the Report had themselves invited:

> Free and sometimes indiscriminate use of words such as 'discovery' has led some critics to the view that English Primary Education needs to be more firmly based on closely argued educational theory. Nevertheless great advances appear to have been made without such theory . . . What is immediately needed is that teachers should bring to bear on their day to day problems astringent intellectual scrutiny.

It is difficult, distanced by time from the late '60s and early '70s, to describe the passions generated by the educational debate which followed upon Plowden. Some schools adopted the imagined Plowden ideal enthusiastically, sometimes, it must be said, without thinking through the implications of the changes which they introduced. Characterised by attractive wall displays, informal seating, classrooms rich in books and materials for children to use in Mathematics, Science, Language, the Arts and Environmental Studies, the schools were busy places of almost continuous activity. How different they were (we who worked in primary schools thought) from the secondary schools described in the Newsom Report of 1963 in which 'children sat through lessons with information and exhortation washing over them and leaving little deposit'.

Where discovery methods were applied in schools which had been designed specifically for child-centred learning, the change was even more apparent. New words and phrases entered the language of education: open plan buildings no longer had classrooms, they had home bases or teaching areas; the maths bay became a resource area; teachers worked in teams; the timetable was replaced by a continually renegotiable programme; staff rooms were regarded as places of retreat but parents' rooms were essential. School trips and real experience supplemented and sometimes even replaced traditional book learning. The new phrases were not so much an indication of the desire to confirm that a revolution in our attitude to young children and their learning had happened, but an attempt to proclaim it.

In trying to paint an accurate word picture of the post-Plowden primary school I have been forced to turn to some old press cuttings. Describing the school in which I worked, Adam Hopkins of *The Sunday Times* wrote:

> The first thing I notice is the quietness – helped along, admittedly, by carpets in many parts of the building. There is a lot of talk but the voices are calm. There is also frequent movement as groups of children rearrange themselves for some fresh topic or activity. But there is little wild running and little silliness. Everybody is quietly getting on. The other thing I notice is the

vividness of the paintings and other artifacts which cover the walls in a rotating display of work in progress.

Against this background I make a note of what is missing. There appears to be no syllabus, no timetable, no formal division of work into school subjects, no specific playtimes. There are no separate classes or classrooms. There is not even a staffroom.

Behind the apparent fluidity of the timetable there is in fact a detailed system of record-keeping so that it is usually possible to say what point each child has reached in each main subject area. This is clearly essential.

The headteacher is discussing passion and revenge with a group of older juniors. He illustrates his points with readings from poets of the First World War. It is strong stuff. The children listen attentively, argue, develop themes. They know about Northern Ireland, the Arab–Israeli conflict, the Christian–Muslim conflict in Beirut. 'People should keep to their own religion and that's that', says one boy. Another thinks religious war is 'just a waste of people'.

Afterwards the headteacher says 'Modern teachers are being crucified because they don't teach facts, facts, facts. But modern children have a lot of facts and it's the interpretation of facts and feelings that makes them civilised.'

I leave the school reluctantly, resolving to return whenever I feel depressed.

It is obvious to me now, though perhaps it was not then, that every revolution will evoke a response from those who fear change or who question the wisdom of moving too far or too quickly from the comfort which traditional practice gives. In addition to the academic scrutiny which the members of the Plowden committee themselves invited, the new approaches to primary education were increasingly attacked by those who felt that standards were falling as a direct consequence of such change.

It could be said, of course, that standards have always been falling. Whatever the base we take, *yesterday's* education always appears to have been golden. A brief dip into history serves to confirm this view:

> . . . there are millions of children in this country who from their babyhood up to the age of 14 are drilled in reading, writing and arithmetic upon a system the result of which is that when they attain the age of 13 or 14 and are finally dismissed from school, they can neither read, nor write, nor cipher.'
> *1904, Sir John Gorst, Secretary to the Board of Education*

> . . . it is a fact that the average boy and girl on leaving school are unable to write English with clearness or fluency or any degree of grammatical accuracy.
> *1912 Conference of Engineering Associations*

> . . . it has been said that accuracy in the manipulation of figures does not reach the same standard which was reached 20 years ago.
> *1925, Board of Education*

> . . . we have received strong evidence of the poor quality of the English of secondary school pupils – we are confronted here with a serious failure of the secondary schools.
> *1943, Norwood Report*

> . . . this House, conscious of the need to raise educational standards at all levels . . .
> *1965, House of Commons, Government motion*

The cry that 'standards are falling' has always been an attractive starting point upon which to base a campaign of retrenchment. And so it was to prove in the late '60s and early '70s. In opposition, and to some extent isolated at a time of political consensus, Conservative educators like Professor Brian Cox and Dr Rhodes Boyson attracted considerable press attention through the publication of a series of 'Black Papers on Education'. They contained articles by a variety of writers (including politicians, and teachers) each of whom had one common aim and purpose – to show that progressive methods in both primary and secondary schools were 'selling children short' and so contributing to the general permissiveness which (they said) was undermining the traditions of British society. That some of the articles were ill-argued, that they lacked style, or that they attributed to schools and teachers almost every ill that mankind was heir to, went unnoticed in the popular press (which reported, usually without reservation, the 'findings' of each Black Paper).

Undoubtedly the 'Black Papers' had the effect which their authors had intended. They slowed down change. Some schools hesitated to implement new ideas, others retreated into the safety which traditional methods appeared to provide. The retreat was understandable. The scandal of Tyndale filled newspapers and TV and radio programmes. The antics of the main protagonists certainly seemed to prove that something was radically wrong in the way our schools were organised. Then, in 1976, while the memory of Tyndale still lingered, Nevil Bennett, a Lecturer at Lancaster University, published a book.

Entitled *Teaching Styles and Pupil Progress* the book was a report based upon field research in North West England. Its findings seemed to show that the claims made by Rhodes Boyson and his Black Paper colleagues were all-too-well founded, ie that formal structured teaching *was* more effective than the methods endorsed by the Plowden Report. Indeed Boyson, now a Conservative MP, welcomed the findings with enthusiasm.

> The study . . . breaks the conspiracy of silence which has shielded so-called progressive education from criticisms that people like the Black Paper writers and myself have been making for years, that standards were falling because of non-structured learning and a lack of curriculum, discipline and order.

It should cause every parent to check what is being done at local schools. If they are filled with progressive rubbish, they should demand from the headmaster and governors that they should return to traditional structured learning so that their children will have a fair chance.

Boyson apart, the findings of report did not go unchallenged. The study was criticised on a number of grounds, principally that it was based on a small sample of children (950) in an area of England (Cheshire) in which informal methods were far from common. Indeed the fact that one of the informal classrooms would have had far less experience of the methods gain in all attainment areas' gave support to those (among whom I number myself) who wondered whether realistic comparisons could be obtained when the schools taking part had no common starting point. The children in the formal classrooms were taught in a traditional way by teachers who were backed by decades of formality. The teachers in informal classroom would have had far less experience of the methods they were employing. New approaches demand new skills. Had the survey been set within an authority (like Oxfordshire, the West Riding of Yorkshire or Berkshire) where progressive methods had been longer practised, the findings might well have been radically different.

What interested me particularly about Bennett's work was another statistic which emerged – that in 1976, considerably fewer than 17% of the primary schools in the study could be described as progressive and that 83% were 'middle of the way' or formal. If this figure applied to the county as a whole then the criticisms which were used to attack progressive methods were quite unjustified; far too few schools had embraced Plowden for them to be having the catastrophic influence which their detractors attributed to them. Indeed, on reflection, it might be said that the 'Plowden Revolution' was a mirage, a revolution that never was.

This viewpoint was confirmed by two other significant pieces of research which followed close upon that of Bennett.

Michael Bassy of Trent Polytechnic found that, far from being radical in their approach, primary teachers were traditional in the extreme. In the schools in his survey, 22 hours a week were devoted to the 3Rs, two hours a week spent on the creative arts and three hours a week given over to other studies.

In 1978 the Primary Survey compiled by Her Majesty's Inspectorate criticised teachers because children were given *too little* autonomy.

> In only 5% of classes was teacher guidance inadequate. In the majority of cases work was prescribed to the extent that there was insufficient opportunity for children to incorporate ideas of their own.

In the face of academic criticism, Black Paper stridency and research like that of Bennett, political intervention was inevitable. It came from an unexpected quarter. The Labour Party, which had played a central part in achieving educational change through Circular 10/65 (see page 15), had become more and more doubtful about the political wisdom of some of the changes it had itself pioneered. In October 1977, James Callaghan, the Labour Prime Minister, spoke at Ruskin College, Oxford. His address implied that schools and teachers were no longer equipping young people to meet the requirements of industry. If industry were unable to draw on a suitably trained and appropriately educated work-force, how could Britain be expected to make its way in the world's markets? Furthermore, if schools could or would not respond to society's needs, it might be necessary to impose a national core curriculum. The speech increased public discussion, and was followed by a series of 'debates' across the country.[7]

The debates may have achieved little but they marked a significant turning point. They indicated that both of the main political parties had reached a similar conclusion. Callaghan seemed to be implying that it was not enough to offer young people a broad liberal curriculum in school, if such a curriculum did not prepare them to face the unthinking anonymity of the factory production line. The suggestion from the Prime Minister that education be geared to serve utilitarian ends was not received with universal approval. Len Murray, the General Secretary of the TUC, reacted angrily:

> It's no good preaching sermons to young people about the value of labour if all they do is to guide a piece of metal into a press and tread on a pedal a hundred times a day . . . It's not the job of education to ensure that young people settle for the status quo.

It would be wrong, however, to think that Callaghan's speech was dreamed up on the spur of the moment, in an attempt to steal some of the educational clothes of his political opponents. Through the 1960s and '70s, subtle changes and reassessments were being made in the relationship between central government (which supplied much of the money) and the local authorities which spent it. The period immediately following upon the end of the war had been characterised by the belief that expenditure on education was not just 'necessary' or 'worthy' but essential: through education, society could and would be transformed. The result was that resources invested in education increased dramatically, even though society in general and the school leaver in particular seemed hardly to be affected. What is more, because education in England (at almost every level) had grown piecemeal there was duplication of programmes, replication, inequality and waste of resources.

The Robbins Report on Higher Education published in 1963 had hinted at reform:

> However well the country may have been served by the largely unco-ordinated activities and initiatives of the past, we are clear that from now on they are not good enough.

The rise in oil prices which began in 1973 resulted in a continuing series of cut-backs on social expenditure. Accompanying these fiscal restraints were demands for greater accountability over the ways in which schools used their resources and fulfilled their broader teaching responsibilities.

The suggested move towards a centrally-determined curriculum, however, was still out of keeping with the spirit of the times. In 1974 John Blackie, Chief Inspector for Primary Schools at the DES was able to write:

> A syllabus, a methodology, a plan of work, an outline study drawn up by some central authority, no matter how enlightened, imposed upon teachers is to be rejected. It is not important how good this programme is. It may be out of date and uninteresting or it may be sophisticated and supplemented by every kind of device and full of interest. It is rejected simply because it *is* a programme, because it denies the initiative, imagination and inventiveness of the teacher in contact with the child.

But even this viewpoint, in keeping with how teachers saw their traditional role as curriculum designers for their own school, was made within an educational context which was changing rapidly.

Sir Edward Boyle, probably the most gifted and perceptive Conservative Education Minister of the post-war years, appreciated that for schools to flourish teachers need to be kept abreast of good practice and encouraged to be responsive to the findings of contemporary research. To achieve this end, Sir Edward had to overcome the parochial instincts of many teachers who felt, with some justification, that no Whitehall mandarin or local authority bureaucrat could possibly understand the problems or needs of the particular children they were teaching.

The vehicle chosen to initiate discussion (and hopefully change) was a School's Council. Established in 1963 it was given the task of finding ways to review and reform the curriculum by encouraging change within the schools themselves. There was no suggestion that the documents which were produced in this process would be used to provide the framework of a centralised curriculum.

The Council was funded by central and local government, its statements were often masterly. Hinting at reform, at the same time they comforted teachers with the reassurance that long-established procedures would remain.

It has long been established in England and Wales that the schools should have the fullest possible measure of responsibility for their own work, including responsibility for their own curriculum and teaching methods which should be evolved by their own staff to meet the needs of their own pupils. We affirm the importance of this principle.

The responsibility of the individual school for their own work is not an exclusive responsibility. It has inevitably to be exercised within a wider framework that takes account of the general interests of the community, both local and national, in the education process.

Statements of this kind were essential if the Schools Council was to receive the support from schools that was needed if the project was to flower. Against this background the Schools Council examined the curriculum in all subject areas and for all age groups. Attention was often drawn to the need to develop continuity within curriculum areas and between school and school. Yet the documents were not prescriptive. They encouraged the production by individual Teachers' Centres of curriculum guidelines. These, while reflecting the findings of academic research, would use local resources to vivify and give meaning to the programmes which were developed. Thus the initiatives of the Schools Council were not devices to control content, change teaching style or to formulate a nationally agreed curriculum. What they did was to provide an opportunity to debate these issues, at the same time giving support to teachers.

A flood of local guidelines flowed from the impetus given by the Schools Council. Among the best were those which posed questions and encouraged individual schools to evaluate their own practice, eg

- What are we trying to achieve?
- What is the present state of knowledge?
- What methods will we employ?
- What resources do we require?
- How much time do we have?
- What evaluation procedure can we employ?

Nevertheless, the work of the Council was not praised by everybody. Sir Alec Clegg, the Education Officer for the West Riding of Yorkshire, accused it of 'drenching and bombarding' teachers with documents. Is there any point, he asked, in filling the jar according to someone else's instincts with stuff that someone else has worked up? Is caring for the child's personal development to be relegated to overtime?

Despite reservations of this kind, the aim of the Council was not diverted. It sought continually to encourage teachers to reevaluate classroom practice – both in curriculum content and methodology. Radical change by Government edict was not thought to be appropriate in England, where teachers had for long seen themselves as equal partners in the process of educational development and change.

By the end of the '70s many elements were fusing together making change in the way schools were run inevitable. Documents from the Schools Council, The Tyndale Scandal, Callaghan's Ruskin speeh, the questions posed by academics like Peters, Dearden, Hirst and Bennett, public anxiety about schools and calls for the accountability of teachers demanded action.

And action was taken. At the same time as Shirley Williams (Secretary of State for Education in the Callaghan administration which was to be defeated in the General Election of 1979) was conducting the 'Great Debate', inspectors from her Department were beginning a process of evaluation of the nation's schools. The Primary School survey was based on direct observation of 542 schools and 1121 classes. Unlike the Plowden Report the survey was concerned with 'the work done by institutions in the classroom' and consciously ignored their 'broader pastoral role'.

The survey examined the way schools were organised but over half of the main document was dedicated to an examination of the curriculum, its planning and continuity, its content, its scope and the standard of work achieved.

The main thrust of the survey was to suggest how primary education could be developed to meet the educational requirements of children as well as the ever-changing needs of society. This was set aginst the teaching and learning which the Inspectorate had observed in their school sample. Were the activities undertaken suited to the capacities of the children? How well did children respond? Was the balance correct?

Although stressing the importance of literacy and numeracy, the survey drew attention to the fact that achievement in basic skills seemed to improve when they were linked to a programme of work which flowed across traditional subject boundaries. It recommended that the curriculum should be examined in the context of national needs and that teachers with specialist skills and particular strengths should be encouraged to use their gifts more effectively. Among the final paragraphs is to be found the following:

> Taking Primary Schools as a whole the curriculum is probably wide enough to serve curriculum needs . . .
> The immediate aim, especially for the average and more able pupils, should probably be to take what is done to a greater length than to introduce content that is new.

Similar surveys were produced for first schools (5–9) and middle schools (9–13).

Two other documents are worthy of mention. In 1980 the Inspectorate published a discussion document *A view of the curriculum*. Defining curriculum as 'all the opportunities for learning provided by a school' it chose, like the Primary Survey to concentrate upon 'the formal aspects of schooling' ignoring but 'not undervaluing other educative influences'.

The document suggested that every school has a common aim, that of helping children 'to meet the basic academic and social demands of adult life' while allowing for the unique differences that exist between child and child. To achieve this aim a curriculum should be formulated which took into account the needs and expectations of society, ensured continuity of the education process throughout the years of compulsory schooling and the importance of the coherence of subject disciplines. In the section devoted to primary education the place of skills was emphasised, as well as the vital part which the teacher plays in children's conceptual development.

The School's Council Working Paper 70 *The Practical Curriculum* was also a response to the 1980 document. It saw its role as 'distinctive'[8] being the

> only national forum where representatives of central government local authorities, teachers organisations, further education and higher education, employers, trades unions, parents, churches and examining bodies meet to discuss the content and process of education in school.

The working paper advocated the need for a visible structure for the curriculum. If what each child takes away from school is its *effective* curriculum, then the starting point of an enquiry should be the right of access which each pupil has 'to different areas of human knowledge and experience'. Like the documents issuing from central Government it listed aims and pointed to the importance of linking teaching to exploration and experience as a means of helping young people 'know the real world'.

The booklet took the form of a discussion document, examining the rationale behind curriculum planning, discussing methods of resolving the problems which often arise when a reshaping of the curriculum is attempted within a school, and identifying ways of monitoring progress and of assessing what has been achieved. Again the emphasis was upon local initiative. Each school was encouraged to define its particular needs and prepare a programme which would best meet them. These needs would be social and emotional as well as academic. Subjects mattered, but only when set against the needs of the individual child within contemporary society.

The above extracts and the documents from which they have been drawn, indicate a shift of emphasis. While they do not mark a return to a prescribed curriculum (like that which applied to schools in England and Wales before 1926), they do signify a subtle change of direction. If the prime task of the teacher is to help children acquire *nationally agreed* learning skills and to deepen their understanding of the concepts which underpin particular academic disciplines, then the way subject matter is presented and used in the classroom requires to be reappraised. This reappraisal will have also to take into account two other elements implicit in current thinking – the need for continuity and coherence both within subject disciplines and between school and school. These are particularly important considerations while differences, rather than similarities, continue to be a characteristic of English education. From diversity there has come richness and innovation: but there has also come failure and lack of achievement.

As we have seen, the move towards a more considered view of the curriculum was hastened by the initiative of central Government, responding to a widely held disenchantment with eduational performance. Hard evidence for this belief was lacking. The public observations and published documents of Government inspectors did not point to falling standards in basic subjects at the primary stage. Certainly the popular press fuelled doubt, focusing as it did upon particular schools which were in temporary disarray, and the failure of a few teachers was applied indiscriminately to the whole workforce.

The 1970s were a period when the parameters of local autonomy enjoyed both by LEAs and schools were discussed. The early years of the 1980s have seen the debate move from generalities to specifics. No longer is the concern a simple alternative – local autonomy *or* centralisation. Today discussion centres upon how much autonomy is appropriate and how, when and where it shall be applied.

The hardening of the position was proclaimed by the DES in *A framework for the school curriculum* published in 1980.

Secretaries of State consider that the diversity of practice that has emerged in recent years, as shown particularly by HM Inspectors' surveys of Primary and Secondary Schools, makes it timely to prepare guidance on the place of certain key elements in the curriculum.

As we have seen, local education authorities responded to these many initiatives from central government. Partly this was because tradition demanded that they should do so. More importantly, however, central government accepted that the LEAs were partners on the difficult path of curriculum change and development. 'Education is a matter of wide interest and shared responsibility' but innovation would never succeed unless the 'professional judgement' of all who worked with children were harnessed. There were sound reasons for this view. Differences occur between teachers, between children, and between various environments in which schools find themselves. Local opportunities *had* to be developed.

This 'sharing of responsibilities' led to the publication of a whole range of curriculum documents by LEAs. The extent to which local authority initiatives divert schools from particular curriculum policies or lead them towards new approaches within the curriculum is, however, impossible to estimate. When a local educational authority demands a policy statement on a particular issue (eg in 1983–84 the ILEA required each school to produce a statement on racism) there may be evidence *on paper* of a change in curriculum emphasis. There may, however, be little or no change in the practices followed by individual schools.

So, gradually and inexorably, the teacher autonomy of the 1960s has been replaced by teacher accountability. The message from central government in the 1980s is unequivocal. Education is too important a task to leave to teachers. There has been hastening of change, a move towards what Kenneth Baker, the Conservative Secretary of State for Education, has called a series of 'benchmarks' appropriate to all schools. These benchmarks would indicate to teachers the things which all children ought to know at a particular stage of their development.

From 1984, a series of broader benchmarks were also finding their way into the schools. Entitled *Curriculum matters* and issued by HM Inspectorate, these 'benchmarks' were presented as discussion documents on particular curriculum areas. Each contains an almost identical preface which states that the overriding aim of the document is to focus upon 'aims, objectives, content, teaching approaches and assessment'.

The curriculum papers also establish one further point. The child at five will be shaped and moulded by the schools he/she attends until he/she is ready for the world of work. It is essential, therefore, that if we are concerned with the end product (the school leaver) continuity and coherence must be the characteristic of the programme which all children follow.

This viewpoint must be set within the wider political context. The belief that all teaching institutions (and the methods they employ) must be evaluated against their effectiveness in producing 'a workforce which industry needs', was one of the central planks of the educational policy of the Conservative administrations of 1979 and 1983. Even Sir Geoffrey Howe, hardly the most strident advocate of the doctrine of market forces, suggested that the education service must be made to 'face this reality'.

To those who, like me, find it difficult to relate the education of the young child to a future market place and to the, as yet unknown, technological changes which the last decade of this century and the first decade of the next will bring, the debate is somewhat arid. I remain unshaken in my belief that the curriculum in the primary years must meet the intellectual, emotional, social and physical needs of the children who are undertaking it and that effective education *has* to be child-centred because it is with children that teachers work. Whilst acknowledging that today's six-year-olds are tomorrow's workforce, what they require of their teachers is the opportunity to begin to learn how to think critically, to question, and to challenge and at the same time acquire the learning skills appropriate to particular academic disciplines.

I would argue that it is the mastery of processes which determine, shape and qualify context (in every academic area) which will be of significant long term value to the child. These thinking qualities are retained long after the catalogue of facts, so long over-valued by some teachers, has been forgotten.

To some extent the advances made in our primary schools in the wake of the Plowden Report have been squandered. It is not just that the ideas which underpin progressive primary methods have been, with a few notable exceptions, poorly articulated. The great majority of practitioners proclaimed their belief in the only way they could – through sound classroom practice.

This inability to 'sell' the product (confident, well-motivated, learning children) contrasted with the methods of those who were prepared to attribute to schools and teachers most of the ills of contemporary society. The long running teachers' dispute which began in November 1984 was to some extent a response to the way the education service had been handled by three successive governments. It was not just about salaries. That the Thatcher Government was able to spin out the dispute into a second year was seen by many as an indication that teachers were somewhat irresponsible. Dare we trust such people ever again with the professional autonomy which they once enjoyed?

Teachers, parents, central government. As we have seen, these three parties are united by a fourth, the local education authority. For many local authorities the early 1980s were difficult years. Having the responsibility vested in them to provide education for the children in their areas, they were faced with two problems: teachers' action and withdrawal of goodwill and a central Government elected with the mandate to restrict public spending. The conflicts which rate-cutting carried fall outside the brief of this book. It is worth noting, however, that just as the teaching force moved from co-operation to conflict, so did many of the local authorities.

Radicalism from a right-wing government spawned radicalism in its opponents. The far left threw its own policies into the pot of educational change and in the process heightened debate and discussion on what schools should teach and how they should teach it.

The topics which caused most concern were in themselves unexceptional. The development of a curriculum which inculcates in children respect for cultures different from their own is surely worthwhile, as is an attempt to correct misconceptions about the role of women in society.

Sadly, when conflict rather than consensus dominates our thinking, rationality tends to be lost. The concentration by some local party caucuses on issues linked to race and sex tended to obscure and confuse the educational debate.

Focusing on such issues also served to provide yet more material for those who argued that schools need to be subject to much stricter government control. For example, it did little to improve parents' view of teachers when schools in one local authority were told to implement a policy aiming to lead young children to an understanding of such things as lesbianism and homosexuality.[9] As John Donaldson, Master of the Rolls, observed in his summing-up in a case involving alleged racism by the headteacher in a Brent infant school:

> . . . a sense of proportion is all important on the part of those who are called upon to judge. A judicial discretion is the essence of real justice. Put at its lowest, a single-minded and unrelenting pursuit of a policy, however right, however important, may be counter-productive in that it may alienate the very people whom it is sought to convert.

Having explored some of the causes of change and identified the areas which will continue to be debated for the next decade, it is perhaps appropriate to try to identify the developments which have occurred in the past 30 years.

Certainly children who start their primary school life in the late 1980s will enter a far richer classroom than did the children I was responsible for on my first day of teaching. To this extent Plowden did have an effect. 'Richness' does not simply describe materials, books, or audio and visual aids, the condition of the furniture or the art reproductions on the walls. The whole pattern and pace of life is more gentle, more in keeping with the needs (emotional, physical and intellectual) of the children. There is, in general, a greater willingness and awareness on the part of teachers that learning, to be effective, needs to be related to the real world beyond the classroom walls. More attention is given than perhaps ever before to the child as creator.

The move away from a curriculum which is mean, meagre and mechanical, remarked upon by Plowden, has continued. In the creative arts, (music making, dance, ceramics, painting, poetry . . .) young people are achieving levels of attainment which, as a young teacher, I would have believed impossible. And standards? Perhaps I should draw upon the comments made by a famous and long serving HMI, the poet Leonard Clark. Writing in *The Times Educational Supplement* in early 1981 he observed

Standards, except perhaps in some of the simple mechanical skills are higher than they have ever been. More of value is done for children and more by them. It is superficial to judge education by false memories and the criteria of the past . . . There must be some schools today where standards *are* lower than they should be, where there is a lack of order and clear purpose, where children are bored and restless. But many of the present-day problems in schools are the result of factors which did not exist in years gone by. The social climate has changed. The world has changed.

It is to the changed world of the primary classroom that I shall now turn.

Notes and references

1 Research findings published by the National Foundation for Educational Research showed that about 10% of children were wrongly placed each year. In 1955 this represented some 78 000 children.

2 This was common practice. In school it had a knock-on effect. The teacher taking the third year 'A' stream moved down to take the equivalent second year class, to prepare them for 'transfer' to the 'finishing' teacher in the following January. The teacher of the second year moved up to 'look after' the old scholarship class.

3 This amounted, according to the critics, not to responsible free choice but its abuse.

4 Following the return of the Conservative Government in June 1987, Kenneth Baker issued a discussion document on the National Curriculum. It suggested that 10 subjects would compose the 'core', and that 90% of school time would be devoted to its implementation.

5 In an interview in the autumn of 1986, Kenneth Baker suggested that benchmarks be established, as indicators of satisfactory educational progress. For 11 year olds, he thought that *Animal Farm* would be appropriate.

6 Each local authority school is responsible to its Board of Governors. The Board is involved in the appointment of teaching staff and in overseeing the finance, curriculum and organisation of the school. It consists of elected representatives of teaching staff, ancillary staff and parents, as well as members nominated by the local authority.

7 The debates, which were conducted on a regional basis, were a cosmetic exercise, attempting to show governmental concern for education.

8 A somewhat over-optimistic view! The council was disbanded by Sir Keith Joseph, Secretary of State for Education and Science in 1984.

9 It is difficult for me as a teacher to help children to empathise with homosexuals and lesbians (even if I thought it were my responsibility to do so) working to a local authority guideline entitled 'anti-heterosexist approaches'. The task of the teacher is to present positive models, not negative ones.

3 Where are we now?

'Is their curriculum humane and realistic, unencumbered by the dead wood of a formal tradition, quickened by inquiry and experiment and inspired not by an attachment to conventional orthodoxies but by a vivid appreciation of the needs of the children themselves? Are their methods of organisation and the character of their equipment, the scale on which they are staffed, the lines on which their education is planned of a kind best calculated to encourage individual and persistent practical activity among pupils, initiative and originality among teachers and to foster in both the spirit which leaves the beaten path and strikes fearlessly into new fields, which is the soul of education?'

This question is taken from the opening section of the report of the Consultative Committee of the Board of Education on the Primary School chaired by W H Hadow. The year was 1931.

If Hadow indicated direction and purpose it was not until the end of the Second World War that such ideals would begin to be realised. The 1930s had seen some reorganisation of state education. Children attended infant school until they were seven. This infant school was sometimes part of a junior school which catered for seven to eleven year olds. Sometimes it was quite independent. At eleven a child might transfer to a grammar or central (technical trade) school or remain in a 'reorganised secondary school'. By 1939 66% of children of secondary age were attending reorganised schools. The remainder were taught in 'all age schools' (ie containing children between the ages of five or seven to 14). The war did little to facilitate reorganisation. As recently as 1949 some 36% of children of secondary age were sharing school buildings with children of primary age.

When set within an historical perspective, it comes as something of a shock to learn that primary education as we perceive it (with children and teachers housed in buildings built or adapted to 'meet the needs of the children themselves') is a recent phenomenon. While it is comparatively easy to accept that in the primary years children have particular and specific qualities and that effective learning is most likely to take place in an environment which meets their intellectual, physical, social and emotional needs, it is much more difficult to define the components which make the learning environment effective.

Schools, after all, are not the only places in which children learn. They acquire a vast amount of information about their world without direct intervention from their parents or their teachers. No structured programme is necessary to teach a baby its mother tongue, to enable the child to master the complexities of sentence construction or grasp the subtle nuances and meanings conveyed in phrase and tone. No blackboards, desks or text books are required, no special buildings: yet even the least able learn.

Notwithstanding such examples, children growing up in a rapidly changing technological society cannot be expected to master all that they require to know if their learning is totally haphazard and unstructured. There must be a framework within which their learning (incidental and guided) is supported and directed. The issue raised by Hadow and developed by Plowden was simply this – is it possible to construct an educational programme which will meet in broad terms the needs of young children and adequately prepare them for secondary schooling, the stresses and strains of adolescence and adulthood beyond?[1]

The way in which our primary schools are organised, both in curriculum terms and in the pattern of the school day, prompts reflection on the range of viewpoints which can be sincerely held when education can be regarded in such humanistic terms. The headteacher who organises a school on 'traditional' lines, the children sitting in rows of desks, following a school day which is divided into periods in each of which teachers deliver packets of information, can argue that his or her educational programme is appropriate. It prepares children for the realities of life.

With equal conviction a neighbouring headteacher might adopt quite a different approach – arguing that only by building a curriculum and a school day around the child can learning be effective and meaningful.

Respect for such differences in viewpoints has produced in England and Wales a range of primary school practice and organisation which cannot be found in any other developed nation. Thus it is almost impossible to define the typical primary school, for although every school staff would maintain that 'they are preparing children for their tomorrow', the approaches adopted to achieve this end are as varied and idiosyncratic as the teachers themselves.

Variety of method and presentation there is, but the variety conceals a common content. Teachers have always tended to be conservative in what they teach.[2] The differences have rarely been about content. They have invariably centred upon process. Of course there have been some minor differences of opinion. Should French be introduced at seven, at nine or not at all? Is it necessary or appropriate to teach spelling? These reservations apart, there is a consensus among all teachers that all children need to be helped towards a broad understanding and appreciation of the world in which they live.

Before attempting to describe the various approaches to learning and teaching which may be found in the contemporary primary school, it would be appropriate to list in the broadest of terms the key elements which lie at the heart of the curriculum. The checklist which follows is not meant to be all-embracing. There will be variations which stem from the background and cultural heritage of the children who are in attendance, from where the school is situated as well as the resources[3] (in quality and quantity) which it receives from the local authority. Furthermore, because education is a gradual process all that my list can indicate is the final goal, not the delicate stages along the way.

These reservations accepted, the core curriculum which primary schools have tried to meet (irrespective of their teaching method or organisation) may be summarised as follows.

LANGUAGE

- to teach children how to speak, read and write fluently
- to teach children how to make use of books, magazines and simple source material (eg on floppy disc and computer tape) and to develop referencing skills (in atlas, dictionary, information books)
- to give children the opportunity to read for information and for pleasure
- to develop in children communication skills, both spoken and written (this includes the development of clear hand-writing and mastery of the appropriate punctuation skills which accompany it)
- to give children the opportunity to express themselves through a variety of approaches including descriptive, imaginative and creative poetry and prose.

MATHEMATICS

- to give children a feeling for mathematics by drawing upon everyday experiences as a means of developing under-standing
- to give children the skills necessary to perform simple

mathematical functions (related to the four rules) without difficulty
- to develop in children an understanding of the concepts which are fundamental to any mathematical enquiry (eg shape and pattern, size, volume, equality and difference, time)
- to give children the skills necessary to solve everyday mathematical problems
- to develop in children the skills of recording and to introduce them to a variety of ways of presenting mathematical ideas (eg graphs, charts, diagrams)
- to develop and extend children's mathematical language

THE CREATIVE ARTS

- to give children experience of the creative arts including:
picture making using a wide range of media
model making using traditional 'waste' and 'found' materials
fabric and collage work
dance and drama, formal and 'free'
music – singing and an introduction to notation through instrumental work (eg using recorder, clarinet and violin)
poetry – listening, choral speaking, writing

ENVIRONMENTAL AND SCIENTIFIC STUDIES

- to give children, throughout their primary years, the opportunity to develop and understand their geographic and historic environment. This would include the study of the area in which they live, its cultural diversity and richness
- to encourage children to explore the natural environment in which they live
- to develop in children an understanding of their bodies, including contemporary health issues such as smoking and drugs
- to offer children experience of simple scientific phenomena

RELIGIOUS/MORAL EDUCATION

- to introduce children to the teaching of the world's major religions
- to give children some understanding of the part played by Christianity in the development of Western culture.

PHYSICAL EDUCATION

- to provide children with the opportunity to master basic skills (eg catching, throwing, swimming) and to play team games appropriate to their age and interests.

A curriculum based upon such a content is to be found in virtually all schools. Missing here are all the intangibles which give the curriculum meaning and purpose, those 'hidden' elements which develop in children a sense of self worth, purpose, self discipline, respect for others and tolerance for religious beliefs and customs which are different from their own . . . in other words all the really important qualities which, if it is to flourish, are required by society! It allows for the development of skills appropriate to each study area and gives teachers the opportunity to explore the specific approaches which are appropriate to particular subject disciplines. It is the kind of curriculum which was advocated by Sir Keith Joseph in March 1985 when he said:

> The primary phase should help pupils to learn to understand themselves, their relationships with others and the world around them; should stimulate their curiosity and teach them to apply it purposefully and usefully; and should develop the foundations for later learning and those personal qualities and attitudes which, if acquired during the primary phase, provide a sound base for what follows.

At first glance this broad agreement on curriculum content does not seem to be reflected in our schools. As we have seen, while teachers and educationalists may agree in broad terms on content, there is much less harmony when the method of its delivery is discussed. Delivery depends first upon the policy adopted by individual schools and, just as significantly, by the individual classroom teacher within each of them. There is one further rider to be added. In as much as a school can be said to have an approach (eg formal, informal, team taught, class or group based, or one where streaming and setting or vertical or horizontal grouping is practised), the degree to which members of staff conform to it very much depends on how the school is led. In this context 'leadership' means more than the drive and direction which comes from the headteacher and senior staff. 'Collective' leadership has become fashionable in some schools; in others radical unionism within a school staff has forced a change in direction and management (even against the wishes and perceptions of its more senior and experienced teachers).

These reservations made, let us now consider some of the different approaches which have been adopted in presenting the curriculum to children. Recent studies (see page 29ff) show that many schools continue to follow an approach to learning which is impeccably orthodox. At the beginning of each year a timetable is prepared and each year group follows a clearly defined, predetermined curriculum. Seven year olds struggle with the four rules in one lesson and cave dwellers in the next, while their eleven-year-old brothers and sisters attempt to master fractions, area and the Victorians. The classrooms in which such learning takes place may *look* very different from those in which I sat as a child 50 years ago (the walls are covered with paintings and there is a computer in the corner, the desks are informally arranged) but the assumption that all learning is determined, ordered and mediated through the teacher is the common thread which links the schools of the 1980s with those of my pre-war childhood.

There are schools in which the practices of the past are even more clearly identifiable. Desks in lines, streamed classes, sets of identical textbooks through which children move from term to term and from year to year all serve to confirm a particular belief. 'Schools are places arranged in such a way that learning can take place. Children learn better within a clear structure which traditional methods impose upon them'. Is it not obviously appropriate, the traditionalists argue, to introduce children of the same age and ability level to new subject areas at the same time? The clever are not held back by their slower classmates, for the bright child and the less able, working with children of their own level, are able to compete intellectually on equal terms.

The formal school, its very formality often proclaimed through uniforms, school prefects and termly reports which show marks and grades, continues to co-exist alongside others which although having almost identical idea on content (eg that young children should be led to an understanding of life in caves and Victorian towns and how to calculate the area in square metres of a field or a carpet) adopt a radically different approach to achieve a seemingly identical end.

'Discovery methods', or 'child-centred learning' were (and continue to be) the phrases most commonly used to describe the methods followed by the informal schools. It would be wrong to think that the Plowden Report was the inspiration for their spread. As we have seen, Plowden commented on what the committee found. Long before Plowden many teachers had rejected traditional approaches to learning because they seemed to deny the way children thought and reasoned, the way in which children could grasp complex ideas, the way in which children dealt with information (not in the neatly boxed subject areas beloved by academics but in broad chunks).

This holistic approach in which the task of the teacher is to respond to the needs, aptitudes and abilities of each individual child in his/her care, drew much of its inspiration from the traditional practice of countless village schools. Small isolated communities did not produce sufficient children to fill village schools with easily ordered year groups. When children entered school the task of the teacher was to measure the strengths and the weaknesses of each child and to use this yardstick as the basis for her teaching. The young and academically gifted worked alongside her older, less-able classmate, at the same time having the opportunity to relate, on a social and emotional level, with her own peers. It was only when the implications of child-centred teaching (the village school at its best) became more widely appreciated that impetus was given to 'informal' or 'open' education.

Advocates of this approach based their practice upon the uniqueness of each individual, drawing their inspiration from a whole range of educationalists and philosophers (Dewey, Montessori, Susan Isaacs, Marion Richardson, A S Neil, Froebel, the McMillans, Bertrand Russell, Pestalozzi, Edith Moorhouse, Robin Tanner and even Rousseau). If, to be effective, learning had to become personalised (made part of oneself – the learner – through direct and vicarious experiences) then each child would need to follow an individualised learning programme. Furthermore, each child learned at a different pace in every subject area and this pace was uneven, reflecting the whole range of influences upon the child external to life in school.[4] So, educational programmes should be based not upon the assumption of commonality of purpose, interest and ability but upon the assumption of individual differences.

Expressed in this way, the thesis has attractions. A child can only learn at his or her own speed from the starting point which has been reached. Furthermore, since learning is something which happens to the individual and not to the group, the value of the individual to the group should be stressed. Group work (often favoured by teachers in informal schools) was used to develop individual gifts and abilities. It tended to replace teacher-imposed activities in which the whole class joined.

Those teachers who worked in such a way were conscious that they were shifting the focus from schooling to learning. If the basis of primary schools was now (to quote Alec Clegg) 'to help each child to walk into his future with firm steps and bright eyes', the primary school classroom should not be a place dominated by the teacher but a place of mutual trust and co-operation. The teacher was seen as a partner in learning – one whose experience and knowledge would be drawn upon, a master alongside willing apprentices.

To teach in this way demanded changes in the way space was organised. If one studies the plans of schools built in the mid-1960s (the Plowden Report contains a number) the impact these ideas made is obvious. Classrooms as such tended to disappear; they were replaced by areas and bays which could be used both for informal workshops and for formal teaching. For despite what its critics may say, formal teaching of the traditional sort from chalkboard and text book, continued to be practised. What was different, however, was that formal teaching was offered when it was required, not because of a timetable.

I am conscious that I have set discovery learning in the past. It is still with us. The schools of the 1960s and 1970s continue to function with the teachers in them adapting their style to meet contemporary needs and expectations. When these methods work well (and I write from experience) such schools are places of tremendous enthusiasm for learning in which the great majority of children make rapid progress in academic studies and in social skills. When they fail they fail because two essential elements necessary for young children's learning have been ignored: security and sense of purpose. When formal schools fail, the same elements are usually found to be missing.

There is a danger inherent in presenting the contemporary primary school in this polarised form. The examples given above indicate a contrast of approach and style. What must be realised is that teachers are rarely confident or certain enough to present themselves as 'progressives' or 'traditionalists'. The successful headteacher is invariably a pragmatist, using such organisation and teaching techniques as is appropriate to the children in his or her care. In schools which may outwardly appear formal, children may be following a curriculum in which traditional academic studies are encouraged, but are integrated under a 'topic' or 'project' umbrella. Such an approach invariably affects the way in which the timetable is followed. For example if history, geography and religious instruction are examined through a topic based upon the life of St Cedd, Gandhi or King Alfred, or an understanding of the local area developed through a study of its changing population and industry, the whole curriculum is likely to be enriched. In developing any topic children will need to refer to books, make notes, write up their findings, draw, model, make maps . . . All of this can and does happen in formal schools. Where they may differ from their informal counterparts is in the amount of time spent on such studies or on the message given to the children and their parents that such activities are incidental to 'real' learning (the mastery of arithmetical or grammatical skills).

Similarly one can find many informal schools where 'setting' takes place for certain activities (eg mathematics and language). 'Setting', the grouping of children of like ability together to follow a particular study or to master a particular skill is little different from traditional streaming. Children in the 'top' set for mathematics quickly come to know that they are more capable than those in the 'bottom' set. The old value systems continue to apply! This is one example of many. I have visited schools where informal methods are practised and in which each teacher has to submit a 'projected' programme for the coming week to the headteacher on each Friday morning together with an analysis of how closely the current week followed the original forecast. Such a structuring of time can be just as restrictive (or supportive) as the traditional timetable.

Neither should it be thought that informal methods necessarily lead to untidy work presented in a poor hand. In one Oxfordshire school in which I spent a day, I saw a nine year old begin a piece of descriptive writing at ten o'clock in the morning. Using black ink and cartridge paper he began to copy out a poem he had himself written, in a beautiful italic hand. At three o'clock he was finished. As he moved from his desk he slipped and spattered the page with blots. His response surprised me, but not apparently his teacher. 'Well, I know how I'll spend tomorrow. Making a copy of my poem!' This little episode happened in a school whose approach to learning was liberal in the extreme. There was no written curriculum, the children were taught in family grouped classes,[5] there were no obvious divisions in the school day. Even playtime breaks and lunch time seemed to be lost in a day of intense and purposeful activity. And yet what had happened – the rejection of an unsatifactory piece of writing – seems somehow more appropriate to the traditional classroom than to its liberal counterpart.

It is because primary schools are difficult to classify in any but the most general terms that the phrase 'mixed methods' is used to describe the practices found in the great majority of them. The differences we find within the schools themselves are a comment on how teachers see their role.

For some, discovery methods continue to dominate classroom practice. The most outspoken supporters of these methods, such as John Holt would argue that learning involves activity, one of the elements most obviously lacking in a classroom dominated by 'chalk, talk and writing'. Teachers, says Holt, talk too much and children all too often listen 'with only a small part of their being, like an adult listening to a boring talk'. For learning to happen 'the learner must continually judge his own performance, become aware of his mistakes. Too often school and non-stop talking turn children into inert and passive learners'.

Viewpoints such as these are challenged by teachers who employ more traditional methods. Activity, they suggest, is not synonymous with learning. Certainly experience helps children in the formation and shaping of concepts but unguarded free activity is likely to be as unrewarding in the long term as a learning programme which never departs from a prepared text book. And is rote learning necessarily in opposition to discovery learning? Might not the mastery of a skill quickly mean that an approach to learning through discovery could be more effectively undertaken? Furthermore if I see my task as a teacher in terms of the development of thinking skills, should I not concentrate upon those procedures which are appropriate to particular academic disciplines? Can I afford to wait for a young child to discover such procedures? Is it not more effective to introduce him to methods in order that such 'discoveries' as are made are appreciated and understood? And if this is seen as intervention by the teacher, is not that happening in every classroom in the land? All interventions constitute a structuring of the child's learning (even in a child-centred classroom).

The intensity of the debate (the flavour of which I have tried to indicate in the preceding paragraphs) and the discovery that every school follows its own daily pattern and its own curriculum, comes as a considerable surprise to educationalists from overseas. The lack of central direction is commented upon. 'How do teachers know what to teach? What if children change schools in mid year or mid career?' The explanation, that there *is* an unwritten curriculum which responds to new demands as they occur (eg the computer revolution of the early 1980s) and that the differences between schools mask even greater similarities is invariably received with scepticism.

Such doubt is to be expected. Not only are there differences between schools within the same local authority area but there are differences in the ways in which each local authority organises its schools. Compare this practice with that of a nation like Sweden where central government, through its agencies and departments, determines such things as curriculum content, methods and content of teacher training courses, and the age groups with which individual teachers may work.

In England and Wales the cabinet minister responsible for Education, the Secretary of State, works through his department. Whenever possible, Ministerial intervention is achieved through negotiation (rather than through detailed legislative powers) and by the use of fiat, circulars and regulations permitted within the legislative framework. Thus he functions as the Guardian of the Education System, the local authorities being the interpreters and initiators of decisions nationally agreed.

Local education authorities (LEAs) vary in size. County Councils have been education authorities since 1888. In areas of high population responsibility for education has been given to some 'first tier' authorities ie district councils within metropolitan regions, such as Salford. In London, education for the ten inner boroughs is the responsibility of the Inner London Education Authority, while the outer ring of boroughs (eg Hillingdon, Bromley) are autonomous education authorities.

The LEAs are responsible for capital expenditure on school premises, furniture and maintenance. Although they are helped to meet expenditure through grants from central government, their monies are prescribed for specific purposes. Thus a local authority can innovate the design of a school building but the overall expenditure must fall within centrally defined cost limits.

Put simply, the duty of the LEAs is to ensure that sufficient schools and teachers are available to provide suitable primary and secondary education to meet the age, needs, aptitudes and abilities of all the children within the area they administer. What determines 'suitable and adequate' is a matter of continuous dialogue between parents, trades unions, professional associations, teachers, administrators and the elected politicians who control the local authority. Differences in provision between one authority and the next can be wide (eg on capitation allowances,[6] the funding of teachers' centres, off-site visits by school groups).

Local education authorities cannot blindly ignore central government policies. In the period 1979–85, restraints imposed by Treasury policy meant that LEAs had less financial freedom. Central government grants were, in real terms, reduced. The effects of such a change can be dramatic. In Oxfordshire, for example, nursery classes (for three to five year olds) were forced to close, nursery placements being an *allowed* but not a compulsory provision. Faced with the impossibility of meeting statutory demands (the provision of education for all children of school age) and non-statutory provision (ie nursery classes) within the finance available to it, the LEA was forced to cease providing for the under-fives.

Local autonomy has also led to variety in the way in which the education system is organised within each LEA. For example in the academic year 1984–85 one local education authority in the North East of England was responsible for the following types of school within the area it administered:–

First schools	5 to 8 years or 5 to 9 years
Infant schools	5 to 7 years
Junior schools	7 to 11 years
Primary schools	5 to 11 years
Middle schools	8 to 12 years or 9 to 13 years
High schools	12 to 16 years or 13 to 16 years
Secondary schools	11 to 16 years

Children over the age of 16 could attend secondary schools, high schools or colleges of further education – another example of piecemeal provision.

These variations were not planned. They were the consequence of the local government reorganisation of 1974. However, they serve to indicate yet another difficulty when describing primary practice.

The variety of local provision highlighted above also serves to provide an interesting comment on how local authorities respond to national initiatives. The establishment of first and middle schools came in the wake of the Plowden Report of 1966. Among its 'Long term recommendations' were:–

a 'There should be a three year course in First School
b This should be followed by a four year course in the Middle School
c There should be national policy on the structure of primary education and on the ages of transfer from stage to stage'

Very few local authorities responded to these recommendations[7] and of those that did a number are in the process of returning to the five to eleven pattern.

For a variety of reasons – some conscious and deliberate, some accidental, some historical and political, some organisational and philosophical – difference rather than similarity appears to be the central characteristic of our primary schools today. For too long we have allowed ourselves to become bogged down in interminable discussions about organisation both within the classroom and outside it.

To a very large extent the way our primary schools develop in the future will be a comment on how much we have learned from the largely fruitless traditionalist *v* progressive debate of the '60s and '70s. To move ahead it will be necessary to try to identify children's learning needs – certain skills in science, history, geography, language and the arts, as well as equally important social and personal ones. The mastery of these skills cannot be neatly prescribed and tied to a particular method. Flexibility within the classroom, the hallmark of the gifted teacher, must find a place in far more of our schools.

Flexibility is a quality which does not flourish easily. Professionals tend to the conservative, and teachers who regard themselves as professionals tend to be more conservative than most. Change can be achieved more effectively when those who are to implement it are well informed. Teaching is essentially a lonely occupation, and a teacher's vision is all too often restricted to the immediate minutiae of school life.

One of the most far reaching developments of recent years, which is still influencing and affecting schools today, came from *Education in Schools, a consultative document.* Published in 1977, by the Department of Education and Science the document suggested that the work of schools needed to be analysed in a 'quantitative' form as well as in the 'subjective and qualitative' way in which it had been measured hitherto. From this suggestion developed the Assessment of Performance Unit (APU) which has to some extent moved discussion away from process to concentrate upon a measurable product.

The Assessment of Performance Unit, a tool of the Government Inspectorate, has concentrated upon the development of tests for national monitoring in English language, mathematics and science. A programme of national assessment began in May 1978 and concerned itself with the standard achieved by 11 year olds. It was extended to 15 year olds in May 1978 and has been subsequently further extended to include language and science.

The reports ('surveys') which stem from the findings of work like that of the APU provide teachers in school with a much broader base upon which to evaluate their current practice. For example, in the teaching of English it was observed that 'inadequate assessment procedures have long been a weakness in schools reflecting uncertainties about aims, objectives and what constitutes progress'. Or again: 'It is suggested that teachers should consider both the test results of the APU and the assessment procedures and relate them to their own teaching aims and objectives and their methods of assessment'.

Not all of the suggestions are as general as these. A comment taken from a mathematics survey observes that too many children have a 'fragile' grasp of decimals, some 33% of 11 year olds considering that a number of 3 decimal places was invariably smaller than a number with 2 decimal places regardless of the digits involved.

Another means of keeping contemporary teachers better informed and less parochial in outlook has been through a range of central and local government books and reports. The most significant of these include the following:

The Bullock Report

A Language for Life was presented to Government in September 1974 and published in 1975. The report sought 'to reflect the organic relationship between the various aspects of

English and to emphasise the need for continuity in their development through school life'. The publication stressed that children should be helped to develop as wide as possible a range of language uses so that they can 'speak appropriately in different situations and use standard forms when they are needed'. Commenting upon the teaching of reading the report takes teachers to task for effectively teaching the mechanics of reading but failing in the process to help children recognise that reading was 'something that people did for pleasure'.

Although Bullock undoubtedly made a major contribution to the teaching of English, there is still much to be done. Both *Primary Education in English* and the APU *Language Performance in Schools* (Report I) stress that in many areas (spoken word, drama, individualised reading) performance must be improved for 'language is our principal means of making sense of our experience and communicating it with others'.

The Cockroft Report

Entitled *Mathematics Counts* the Cockroft Report was published in 1983. It emphasised that there was no one style appropriate for the teaching of mathematics, for

> this is neither desirable or possible. Nevertheless . . . mathematics at all levels should include possibilities for exposition by the teacher, discussion between teacher and pupils and between the pupils themselves, appropriate practical work, consideration and practice of fundamental skills and fortunes, problem solving including application of Mathematics to everyday situations, investigational work.

Mastery of mathematics, according to Cockroft, gives children a powerful means of communication, a way of representing, a way of explaining and a way of predicting. At the primary level, the mathematics curriculum should, therefore, equip children with the skills and language of number, enrich their aesthetic and linguistic experience, provide them with the means of exploring and commenting upon their environment, and develop their powers of logical thought.

It should be noted that Cockroft did not concentrate upon arithmetical skills (the 3rd 'R' of the Victorian school). Like Bullock, it presented this area of human experience as a pleasurable, worthwhile activity helping 'each pupil to develop appreciation and enjoyment'.

The message implicit in the Cockroft Report is that mathematics, like English, is a language for life. To be effective, children's mathematical experience needs to be rather more wide ranging and demanding than presently seems to be the case. Although computers and calculators have become an accepted part of mathematical teaching their presence in the classroom, should not be taken as evidence *per se* of 'up-to-dateness'. Mathematics is not just about developing facility for number: it is essentially a subject which has links with all other curriculum areas and should never be taught in isolation.

Bullock and Cockroft served to indicate the direction that progress might take. They still serve as a yardstick against which to measure each individual school. One recommendation advanced by both reports was that each primary school should have a 'teacher-consultant' who would act as leader in these specialist subject areas. The movement towards subject specialism within the primary school has already begun. It marks, if implemented to any extent, a fundamental change in how primary schools will in the future be organised.[8] Justifying the appointment of teacher consultants, Sir Keith Joseph said to the delegates at the 1985 CLEA conference:

> There are advantages for everyone, and most of all for the pupils, in making the transition from class teaching in the primary school to specialist teaching in the secondary school a gradual rather than a sudden one.
> It follows that the way in which the upper years of

junior schools are organised should be seen – just as already happens for pupils of the same age in middle schools – as part of the process of securing good continuity between the primary and secondary phases. There is another important reason why the oldest primary pupils should not be taught exclusively by their class teacher. In most primary schools certain teachers have, or can acquire, special strengths which ought to be made available, on a rational division of labour, to children outside their class and to their colleagues.

The avalanche of publications in the late 1970s and early 1980s, including the Department of Education's *Curriculum papers 5 to 16*, have served one other purpose. They have helped to defuse the arguments about teaching style and concentrate attention upon content and delivery.

Local educational authorities have also provided valuable information on the effectiveness and current practices of our primary schools. In early 1986 the Research and Statistics branch of the Inner London Education Authority presented a study which had taken three and a half years to compile, based upon the schoolwork of 2000 pupils in 50 randomly selected primary schools. During the period of the study each child's progress was measured in eight subject areas including mathematics, reading, writing and oracy. The study confirmed findings which had been highlighted in earlier research, for example that schools tend to be more successful if leadership is purposeful and teachers cooperate in the implementation of an agreed policy. It also contained the following findings:

- Children performed better when the day was structured in some way. In effective classrooms the teacher provided clear direction but allowed children some autonomy.
- Children performed best in a work-centred environment and one where teaching was intellectually challenging.
- Record keeping to monitor the children's progress is vital.

● Parental involvement and interest contributes significantly to children's learning.

One particularly interesting observation emerged from this research: that social background (rather than cultural/ethnic differences) confirms inequalities of opportunity. For example, it was found that seven-year-old children in the sample from non-manual homes had a reading age 16 months ahead of children from manual and unskilled homes. This is often a critical gap, for unless it is bridged, the child from the economically poorer background is never likely to cope adequately with schooling. Observing that the effective school can help the disadvantaged child to make use of the opportunities schools provide, the report also commented upon the scale of the contribution which the effective school could make. It calculated that the difference between a good school and a bad one accounts for about 20% of the variation in children's progress (between the ages of seven and 11) in reading, writing and mathematics. Furthermore, schooling plays a far more significant part in academic progress than does race, sex or background.

All of the documents and reports to which I have referred in this chapter serve to throw light upon the contemporary primary school and to provide material upon which to speculate about future developments. Towards the end of 1986 yet another report appeared. It contained the findings of the House of Commons *Select Committee on Education and the Arts*, chaired by Sir William Straubenzee. Observing that primary education is the 'foundation upon which all subsequent stages of education are built' the committee accepted (as do the majority of contemporary documents) that some curriculum guidance to schools is necessary and appropriate. To achieve this end it envisaged a series of documents similar to the DES *Curriculum guidelines*. These documents would form the basis of development plans worked out by each individual school.

Curriculum guidance

The mid-1980s has been characterised by a shift in emphasis in the educational debate. Discussion on approach to curriculum (should it be progressive, traditional, mixed) has been overtaken by a more crucial issue. What will the curriculum contain and who will determine its contents? To some extent this has united those who work in the schools. The imposition of a curriculum from above will not mean, if assurance given by politicians is to be believed, that teachers will be prevented from delivering it in the way they think most appropriate. In other words each primary school will continue to reflect its own individuality.

The move towards a more formalised contract between schools and the broader society they are there to serve has wide support from the major political parties. Such doubts as exist stem from the power which curriculum control gives to the curriculum designers (a topic to which I will return in later chapters).

Nevertheless it must be realised that the energy we now devote to curriculum content has tended to overshadow and obliterate the debate about curriculum delivery with which this chapter has also been concerned.

I have suggested that the curriculum content of our primary schools has in broad terms always been 'agreed'. Should it be encapsulated within a nationally agreed document the question of how that content can best be delivered will once more return to plague us. For some schools the central guidelines will be interpreted through a carefully structured timetable. Without doubt there will be schools who see the guidelines as indicators of direction and in which child-centred learning will take precedence over externally imposed guidelines.

To suggest that we must look at today's schools against an ever continuing and unchanging debate about curriculum content and delivery may seem unhelpful. In the early 1970s the ILEA commissioned an in depth report into the school of which I was headteacher. I quote from its conclusion:

In sum there are certain defining characteristics of the school which emerge from our study. In the first instance, it was in many ways conventionally arranged: the teachers and their groups spent most of their time within their home bases where provision was made for most types of activity. Within a fairly conventional framework however, the organisation demonstrated its flexibility – neither teaching arrangements, nor use of space, nor grouping of pupils were static, but frequently discussed and open to change. Such flexibility was easier to foster given a basic consensus amongst the staff. This provided a framework within which individual differences and proposed changes could be discussed. It was a consensus based on a common attitude towards the children as the interviews and classroom recordings show. The teachers wished to create a friendly and supportive atmosphere in which children learnt to trust the teacher and each other. Our information on amounts and type of interaction would suggest that such an atmosphere did exist.

Above all our information would dispel the notion that such a learning situation was a 'free-for-all' with no discernible structure. The structure of the day emerged from group discussions between teachers and individual children at various points throughout the day, and between the teachers themselves at their daily lunch-time meetings. It was therefore a structure which was *continually negotiated* on a daily or weekly basis aiming to maximise the enjoyment and interest of learning in the present. Such a structure is in contrast to a structure which, once negotiated, is subject to little questioning, which orders activities on a termly or a yearly basis, and which has a declared interest in the future than the present. In the words of the headmaster, this is a school which is 'more interested in a child's today than his tomorrow – in where the child is now in relation to where he was, rather than in relation to our expectations of where he ought to be'.

What was true in the 1970s has equal relevance to the present and the future. However well we make plans for our children tomorrow we can only move from the point they have reached today. And the methods employed to ensure that movement occurs? Surely that question will continue to be debated for as long as there are children in schools and teachers there to teach them.

Notes and references

1 The Plowden Report was unequivocal in the view it presented: 'The preparation for being a happy and useful man or woman is to live fully as a child.'

2 On the whole, the great majority of teachers have always sought to avoid contentious contemporary issues. Topics related to such things as race, class and gender owe their appearance in schools to political rather than professional action. Political decisions at local authority level can demand, for example, that a school policy on anti-racist attitudes be formulated and initiated or that governors representing minority cultures be appointed to each governing body. The effect of such measures designed to 'raise awareness' can be to significantly alter curriculum content and make teachers appear to be far more radical than they actually are.

3 These vary tremendously. In the financial year 1983/4 £57.18 was spent (on books and equipment) on each primary child in ILEA, £22.72 in Richmond (London Borough), £40.42 in Sheffield (Metropolitan District), £36.37 in the County of Nottingham and £18.97 in Shropshire. In Wales the figures ranged from £33.08 (Powys) to £19.66 (Dyfed). These figures are based on returns made to the Dept of Education ROI EDUCATION FORMS, COLUMNS 18, 19 and 21.

4 For example, on the one hand, tensions within the family (marital breakdowns, illness, unemployment, financial problems) and on the other all the information and knowledge which the child has acquired from his/her experience of living.

5 When a school is family groups, children work in mixed age classes (eg 5–7, 7–9, 9–11 or 5–8, 9–11). By reducing competition between children within the same age group, the teacher can

follow strategies appropriate to each child, flexibly arranging the class groupings to reflect individual academic, social and emotional needs. Such needs are not neessarily age related or constant.

6 The amount of money allowed per child per year by the LEA to the school, for expenditure on books and equipment. The amount granted per child is usually determined by age, ie allowances for children of nursery and infant age are lower than those for junior children (7–11); at the secondary stage (11–16) the allowance is increased, reaching a maximum for children in the 16–18+ age groups. (See also page 48)

7 In January 1983 there were 610 middle schools, many of which will have disappeared through reorganisation by September 1988.

8 See also page 91, Chapter 5.

4 Teachers – professionals or artisans?

'Teaching offers an escape route for the more fortunate members of the working classes.' This view was expressed forcibly but politely to students who were being prepared to teach in state schools. The year was 1952, I was one of the students.

I remember that the lecturer went on to develop his thesis – that to teach one required an acceptable level of numeracy and literacy, some basic classroom skills, an academic interest or 'enthusiasm' which could be passed on to children and some awareness of basic psychology. Through exposure to children on school practice, through attending lectures, writing essays and being reasonably responsible in college we would (he said) be ready, in two years, to enter teaching.

No-one challenged the assumptions which ran throughout the lecture. Teaching *did* provide an opportunity for young people to move up the social scale. In the 1950s teacher training furnished a relatively easy route to the secure status of superannuated salary earner. Two years of training compared favourably with the minimum three years it took to acquire a degree. While there was such a difference in the length of time it took to acquire qualifications, many working class youngsters who had achieved good grades in the sixth form tended to view a course in teacher training as marking the limit of their ambitions.

In the 1960s teacher training was extended to three years

and a B Ed degree replaced the teaching certificate. When this happened teaching no longer offered a short cut to secure (if indifferently paid) employment. With grants available to all who could gain entry to university or polytechnic, initial teaching training courses came to be filled, in part, with young people whose 'A' level grades were not high enough to gain entrance on conventional university course.

This is not to suggest that today's B Ed student is less competent than his or her counterpart of the 1950s or early 1960s. Rather it points to the fact that there has been a subtle change in the composition of the teaching force. Today's student teachers and young graduates undoubtedly represent a broader spread of social background – and this is to be welcomed. The belief, sincerely held by many of my working class contemporaries, that teaching was a much better job than many of the others which were open to them, no longer applies. Today's teaching force probably contains a rather higher proportion of workers who would prefer to be employed elsewhere than was the case 30 or 40 years ago. For the majority of students to succeed and become a teacher is not the dream it once was; nor does the possession of the title 'teacher' enjoy the prestige with family and friends which was once common. Today teaching is a job like any other, its reward determined by market forces, its value measured by the salary it commands.

We cannot, of course, live in the past. Times, attitudes and expectations change. Students entering a polytechnic this September will be trained more rigorously and be wider read than students of my generation.

Nor should it be assumed that the young teachers of 30 years ago were all aspiring members of the working class. There were then, as there are today, young people from other groups who, irrespective of academic ability or social class, felt that through teaching they would be serving future generations.

This projection of a caring service in which adults helped children to master the skills necessary to live in a society growing ever more complex, encouraged teacher-trainers in the immediate post-war years to be somewhat self-indulgent and to suggest that teachers were members of a profession. In effect, if it *was* a profession it was a profession in name only (a point made indirectly by my lecturer who studiously avoided use of the word).

The myth is still with us. Teaching continues to be described as a profession, particularly by the leaders of the various trade unions in supporting claims for higher pay and better conditions for their members. But *is* teaching a profession? Does teaching meet the requirements integral to any profession. I think not, for the following reasons:

1 'PROFESSIONAL' IMPLIES THE POSSESSION OF SPECIALIST KNOWLEDGE AND AUTHORITY

The professional person has knowledge, and the experience of applying it, which is not possessed by the great majority of the population. We go to a solicitor for advice beause he knows the law; to a doctor because she can interpret symptoms. We consult the professional when help of a specific nature is required, often when the situation in which we find ourselves contains an element of crisis. 'I must sell this house, resolve this will'. 'I have this acute pain in my side'. The professional responds to clearly articulated needs. This element is lacking in teaching. Children are sent to school, with no specific need. The resulting 'contract' between teacher and taught is therefore loose and far from explicit.

We have been developing, since the mid-1960s, an ever more highly trained teaching force. Longer training has resulted in students taking courses which are ever more demanding. Certainly subjects are studied at much greater depth than when I was trained. And yet is the teacher's knowledge exclusive? Parents who have watched their children grow and develop are just as likely to have insights into the development of their child as the teacher who has taught for a couple of years. Indeed, a young mother's intuitive feelings may be far more in keeping with her child's needs than the academically weighted perspective of the middle aged teacher inexperienced in parenthood.

It is significant that recent government policies have sought to give parents more power and influence in school – to elevate parenthood and, by giving parents' views more weight, counter the claim to exclusiveness so often made by the teacher.

2 MEMBERS OF A PROFESSION SEEK TO PURSUE THE INTERESTS OF THEIR CLIENTS

Teachers have always been somewhat confused as to who is their client. Is their client the child? If so, then the child's interests and rights should be defended, and meeting the child's needs should be of paramount importance. The child, however, is a minor, the legal responsibility of his/her parents or guardians. If the parents are the client and we, as teachers, pursue the parents' needs, wishes and aspirations, may not this obstruct and confuse the working relationship we have with individual children?

Thus to consider a professional-client relationship when relating professionalism to teaching is made even more difficult since it is impossible to view this relationship in personal terms. The client of the teacher is society and the responsibility of the teacher is to act for and on behalf of society. If we adopt this standpoint authority lies not with teachers but with those who define society's expectation of schools and of the teachers who work in them. It is in this area, accountability, that much of the recent debate on the education service has centred.

3 A PROFESSION HAS JURISDICTION OVER ITS MEMBERS

As we have seen, teachers have very little authority over what they do or how they do it. There is no formally established council equivalent, for example, to the British Medical

Council or the Law Society, which controls entry to teaching. Teachers are trained in institutions which run courses approved by Central Government. Once qualified they are certificated to teach by the Department of Education and Science and can then be employed by local authorities (often on the recommendation of lay boards of Governors).

Instead of gaining entry by qualification to a professional body, teachers, on becoming qualified, may join (if they so wish) one of six unions. Each union follows its own policy, makes its own rules and regulations (and tends to bicker with the other five). As a consequence there is no one body which speaks for teachers or presents a considered and constructive view of education.

Although there has been considerable support for a Teachers' Council, the proposal has made little headway. For it to do so the major unions would have to relinquish much of their power. Until a Teachers' Council is established, teachers will continue to lack the organisational structure through which to control the entry, training and practice of the members of their 'profession'.

While failure to establish an effective Teachers' Council supports the view that teaching cannot be regarded as a profession, the establishment of such a Council would be fraught with administrative difficulties. There are comparatively few doctors of medicine, barristers, solicitors, or clerks in holy orders. By comparison there are many, many teachers. A profession tends to have few members, each member possessing esoteric knowledge which sets him or her apart from their peers. Could a Council be established which could cope with the demands made upon it by a multitude of members? To whom would such a Council be answerable?

4 A PROFESSION HAS DEFINED AND ENFORCEABLE ETHICAL STANDARDS

Apart from respect for the law, there are no defined standards which teachers have to follow. As a matter of common courtesy, for example, a teacher would avoid giving private coaching to child in a colleague's class. But this unspoken rule does not prevent teaching a child from a neighbouring school – 'filling the gaps' which a fellow 'professional' has left in a child's mathematics or English grammar.

Such considerations, however, pale into insignificance against the effects of the industrial action which plagued schools in England and Wales from the Autumn of 1984 onwards. 'Withdrawal of goodwill' caused many people (myself included) to question whether teaching could ever be viewed as a 'profession' when the ethics which are central to teaching (responsible and thoughtful care for the young) could be so readily ignored by so many teachers.

The inaction of an unsympathetic government and an intractable Secretary of State did nothing to resolve the conflict over the pay and working conditions of teachers. Nevertheless the chaos which resulted in our schools (a result of bull-headed intransigence on both sides) did not suggest professionalism either from politicians or teachers. The long term consequences of the dispute are difficult to estimate.

However, one thing is crystal clear. The teachers' unions adopted a policy of industrial action and employed techniques appropriate to an industrial conflict. As a consequence staff rooms became divided, personal relationships shattered and effective schooling was destroyed.

At the same time as this was happening teachers demanded to be treated 'as professionals', scornfully ignoring the view, repeatedly expressed, that the disruption of children's education for so long a period was hardly the behaviour that one might expect from members of a 'profession'.

The retreat from professional standards which marked the period of industrial action has given new impetus to those politicians and administrators who seek to define the teacher's role. The draft agreement of November 1986 between the teachers' unions and representatives of the local educational authorities indicates the extent to which 'formalism' is beginning to replace the informed individualism which once characterised English schools. Thus in *The Duties of Teachers*, (Draft agreement, November 1986) we find the following.

1.1 Basic contractual requirements:

The basic contractual requirements of the jobs of the different grades of teacher are defined in Appendices 1 (a), 1 (b), 1 (c) and 1 (d) and in Appendix 3.

1.2 School-based job descriptions:

1.2.1. Each teacher shall be given an individual job description specifying his or her particular responsibilities. The job description shall be consistent with the contractual duties laid down in this agreement. The job description should be reviewed annually, and more frequently if circumstances so require and where necessary amended, subject to any agreed requirements of consultation and notice and have regard to the teacher's previous role, experience and potential.

1.2.2. In preparing the job description the head teacher shall ensure that no teacher shall be given a job description which requires him or her to undertake duties which in combination cannot reasonably be discharged.

1.3 Voluntary activities:

There are some activities in which teachers engage over and above what shall be contractually required. Those activities are greatly valued and should be regarded as part of the full professional role.[1] No such additional work shall be taken as implied agreement to, or modification of, the individual contract, nor shall such additional work, however widespread among teachers, be taken as implied variation of the terms of this agreement.

The draft agreement outlines, in great detail (11 sections and 33 sub-sections) the hours which teachers shall work, contractual limitations upon teachers' workload, the grade structure within schools and methods of appraising teachers as well as details on pay, negotiating machinery and the responsibility of the employers.

Such an agreement may in political terms be the only way out of the impasse in which the teachers find themselves. Such an agreement, however, has clearer links with the factory floor than the consulting room. If teachers use the methods of the artisan to achieve satisfactory wage levels (to which I agree they are entitled) it is only reasonable for society, through its elected representatives, to view them in these terms and define for teachers their role and function.

Thirty-five years ago my lecturer did not see fit to use the word profession. He was Welsh and preferred the gentle language of the valleys to the prescriptive phrases of the academic. For him teaching was a 'calling' – a career which, though academic, had at its core the concept of service to others. I appreciate that this view is somewhat unfashionable and would gain little support from the majority of teachers who were at the centre of the disruptions of recent years.

Yet it is a view which needs to be restated. There is now a need to rekindle the idea that teaching is a vocation which makes a whole series of complex demands. Not all of these demands are quantifiable and measurable or will rest easily within a neat job description: some will stem from anxieties about children's academic progress, some will centre upon their social and emotional welfare.

If teachers are to merit the title of 'professional', using the word not in the narrow context outlined above but in the sense of somebody who in their employment performs a task well, teachers will need to regain the confidence of the public. It will mean putting aside the confrontation, frustration and bitterness which has characterised the relationships of teaching unions, government, parents and local authorities. Teachers will also have to reassess the part they have to play in the education of *all*[2] the children in their care. This reassessment could cover a number of inter-related areas.

The staffroom

Each teacher must be aware of what his or her particular school is about – its rationale, its purpose. If this is to happen then there must be far greater participation than there has been hitherto by all members of the school staff in the establishment of general philosophy and purpose of the school. The consensus thus established is much more likely to create an environment which reflects the *now* in education; it will certainly be more effective than either radical revolution, deschooling or free schooling.

We must have schools staffed by people who are intellectually alert, who are able to change methodology and doctrine to meet the needs of today's children. It requires courage and support from sympathetic colleagues to admit that the things that have been happening in classrooms or schools over the past 20 years have been wrong, pigheaded or simply inefficient. It is pertinent to observe that education is about an emotional response to real situations – not simply about facts. That teachers – young, middle-aged, and those near retirement – can be asked to express how they really feel about curriculum developments can only be for the good.

I believe that such a sharing will lead to each school establishing its own targets: not narrow targets like those listed by well-intentioned politicians but much broader-based priorities. In the two schools in which I spent much of my working life (one as head, one as assistant teacher responsible for physical education) the broad aims were almost identical and may be summed up as follows: the creation of a living community of children in which the Arts, music, painting and poetry flourished; where social awareness came before selfish intolerance; where the written and spoken word was valued as a means to a more distant educational end rather than as an end in itself; where understanding of number was regarded as more important than the ability to manipulate figures.

Without doubt, the biggest change in primary education in

the past ten years has been the proliferation of guidelines and schemes of work. Guidelines, of themselves, are not enough. I have learned from many discussions with primary teachers in schools in Sweden, Yugoslavia and Bulgaria (where centrally imposed guidelines are used) that guidelines tend to confine. In indicating direction they serve also to stress content and method. In indicating content and method they spawn 'approved' material of all kinds which, if used, serves to protect the individual teacher from any criticism which might arise were he or she to follow a more tangental or personalised approach to meeting curriculum goals.

Schools can only succeed when there is dialogue within the staffroom – a dialogue which leads to a broad agreement on the direction in which the school should move, both in the present and in the future. This does not of necessity call for a middle way between the extremes of egalitarianism on the one hand and élitism on the other. What it does demand is a policy based on staffroom agreement which can be accepted by teachers and parents as being appropriate to meeting the needs of the children which the school is there to serve.

The alternative to consensus is often disaster. When a staff divides, the school dies. One of the saddest effects of the radical trade unionism of recent years is that it has divided teacher from teacher, head teacher from staff, teachers from ancillary workers, schools from parents. The divisions (which in the main centred upon the appropriateness of particular forms of industrial action) made it virtually impossible for school staffs to discuss those things which really mattered – the education of the children in their care.

The classroom

What sets the true teacher apart is the ability he or she has to relate to children with thoughtfulness, concern and love. The ability to organise a classroom, a group or an individual child, to structure experience so that learning not only occurs at the moment of teaching but remains; the sensitivity to perceive the world from a child's perspective, the understanding to build for tomorrow upon the child's present, and to know and appreciate a child's weaknesses and strengths – these are the skills which are the basis for a teacher's claim to 'professionalism'. Such skills and abilities are not the prerogative of a particular sort of teacher or of a particular style of teaching – nor are they to be found only in teachers who work with the youngest children in our primary schools. They are most likely to be found in classrooms where teacher, child and parent trust each other. In many schools the most dramatic effect of the teachers' action was the shattering of this unspoken contract between teacher, parent and child. Professionalism thrives on trust. We who teach should not expect to be valued as 'professionals' if we cannot be trusted.

The individual teacher

The task of the teacher within the primary school is essentially to be a creative initiator of situations from which and in which children will learn. To achieve this goal teachers need to be academics in the broadest sense of the word; not simply a graduate in a traditional discipline but someone who is able to use the richness of our cultural past and the opportunities offered by our multicultural present to challenge children's thinking and, by so doing, to open up for them avenues of discovery.

Within the community

We live in the age of the job description. The question 'What do you teach?' presupposes a neat academic answer – history, mathematics, language. In my experience the unexpected response 'children' causes the questioner to smile in puzzlement and change the subject. Yet we who teach in primary schools need continually to remember that it is with children that we work. The strength and the uniqueness of the English primary school has been based upon a tradition of generalist training and generalist teaching. We might, as individuals, have specific interests in poetry and literature, mathematics or art, history or science, and we might well seek to share our enthusiasm with the children we teach. This, however, has never been our central concern. We have taught children across the curriculum, at the same time carrying broad pastoral responsibilities. Put another way: we have sought to teach children by establishing a close personal contact with them and by developing an understanding of the social conditions in which they live. The quality of 'education in the round' is to be found at its most developed in the small village school where the teachers so often become an integral part of the community in which they work.

England and Wales are no longer rural countries. The great majority of their citizens live in towns and cities. Fortunately the belief continues to be fostered by the great majority of heads that teachers must never ignore the community beyond the classroom walls. At its simplest this involvement is little more than preserving the bridge which exists between home and school, giving support to children and their parents at moments of personal crisis (like a death, or the break up of a family). At its most complex and demanding, involvement may mean taking action to protect a child against cruelty and neglect.

If supporting parents and children is important for members of the indigenous community, how much more important it is to help children and parents from minority cultures to understand the nature of school and schooling. To care for children fully, teachers need to develop an appreciation of the expectations, hopes, tensions and anxieties of their parents (whatever their roots). Where such an understanding develops the teacher is more able to relate to the child in the classroom. Of course the additional work which such an outward-going policy requires will make demands upon the teacher's time. The realisation that we teach children more effectively if we understand them fully and set them against the social and cultural conditions in which they live and grow, places an expectation upon the teacher which cannot be prescribed by contract.

The prestige enjoyed by many of our primary schools, the way in which they are valued by the parent body, has been built upon the work of teachers who have realised that they have a role both within the school and outside it. To help fashion the 'whole child' they have needed to *know* the whole child.

A teacher who regards his work in this way, who sees his task as being not merely an overseer of academic progress but a mature adult who watches over and helps a child to find personal identity in an ever more complex and fast moving world may deservedly claim to be considered doing work worthy of professional status.

So *are* teachers professional? Undoubtedly teachers fulfil an important function in contemporary society. The teachers' organisations argue, quite rightly, that teaching is becoming ever more demanding. Children brought up on a diet of TV and video are no longer as tractable and easy to control, as they once used to be, even in the younger classes of the junior school.

Children seem to have changed. So too have the subjects which the primary school teacher is expected to cover. The basic '4 Rs' of my teacher training (reading, writing, arithmetic and religion) have expanded considerably. It's an ill-trained infant teacher nowadays who cannot lead a lesson on creative dance, use a video recorder, insert a floppy disc, be aware of the latest approaches to reading and number and be ready to explain to her class the nature of Diwali and the Festival of Lights.

To an extent it is this explosion of the curriculum which has contributed to the moves towards a more standardised, coherent curriculum for our schools and to demands that teachers be subject to a system of appraisal.

Appraisal has always happened in schools. Teachers were

promoted because, in the view of the Inspectorate and on the advice of their peers (usually the headteacher), they were effective classroom teachers.

Appraisal is attracting more attention because (as we have seen in Chapters 2 and 3) accountability has become politically fashionable. We are told, for example, that if teachers are made accountable standards will be raised. Quality will return to teaching. Employers will be given a yardstick against which to measure teachers. Parents will, in consequence, have more faith in state schools.

A number of experiments have been set up to try to establish a satisfactory method of appraisal. One approach involves each teacher undertaking a form of self-evaluation. Helped by an external observer (the head of the school or a senior member of staff) the teacher is invited to determine his/her strengths and weaknesses and to list priorities for personal development. These priorities, for example, might be expressed through a request to teach a different age group or to be given time to take a specific course. This self-evaluation (which would be undertaken by every member of the school staff) would then be set against priorities within the school. How can the needs of individual teachers be met and their strengths harnessed within the broader concerns of the school?

Some local educational authorities encourage self-evaluation or informal monitoring each year, the exercise culminating every three or five years in an in-depth review. Why are we doing what we are doing? Is our curriculum and organisation still relevant? What changes do we need to make? What strategies can we employ to realise our own goals?

If a more formal system of appraisal is adopted (as has happened in some part of the United States) to evaluate teachers throughout their career, certain significant problems will need to be resolved. What will be the composition of the evaluating panel? Will the panel be independent of schools and answerable to the local authority through its inspectorate, or directly to the DES? On what basis will a teacher be appraised? Every class and every school is different. How does one compare the class work of a teacher in Tunbridge Wells whose five year olds all come from homes where books are common, to that of a teacher in a multiracial school in St Paul's, Bristol? Should we, in any event, be appraising teachers as individuals? Is not a school a collective in which individualised approaches are often sacrificed in the interests of the larger teaching team? And who will bear the cost? Is the money and time which will be spent on preparation, classroom observation, post appraisal interview, intepretation, evaluation and implementation to be taken from the general education budget? If appraisal leads to the creation of a new bureaucracy which consumes money which would otherwise be spent on resources for children, is such formalised procedure likely to be beneficial?

The need for formal assessment has already been conceded by teachers. The proposed agreement between teachers and their employers (November 1986) states that 'the performance of teachers on entry grade will be monitored and assessed throughout their service' (on that grade). The agreement indicates how, through a series of interviews, reports and assessments spaced over two years, entry grade teachers can become teachers on main professional grade (which carries with it an appropriate salary increase).

It could be that this development marks the beginning of a teaching force which is professional in reality as well as in name. Control over the quality of work within each classroom has until now been left almost exclusively to the headteacher with occasional support from the local and national inspectorate. Monitoring of the practice of individual teachers, together with a shared responsibility for the work of each school, may result in a raising of the self esteem of teachers.

A national system of appraisal might also encourage the teacher unions to unite in a demand for the establishment of a Teachers' Council which could be made responsible for regulating entry to teaching and for establishing a code of conduct (particularly important when teachers are able, in appraisal schemes, to judge their colleagues). Such a Council could also co-operate with institutions which train teachers and take part in the validation of their teacher training courses. It might also take on the role of initiator of research and the evaluation of material.

Although the developments outlined above might go some way towards encouraging parents and politicians to regard teachers as 'professional' much more will need to be done to repair the damage caused by the years of industrial dispute. Fred Jarvis of the National Union of Teachers has already hinted at the fundamental difficulty which arises when the professional is set within tightly prescribed guidelines. Speaking at the Union's annual conference (Easter 1987) he reflected on the imposition of a contract upon teachers by central Government. This contract, imposed unilaterally in March 1987, requires teachers to work 1265 hours, 'allocated reasonably to 195 days a year . . . at the direction of the head teacher or local authority.'

Working to such a contract will undoubtedly cause changes in the climate of school life. Personal commitment will tend to be replaced by the rule book and the clock. As Mr Jarvis observed 'The old days of teachers being trusted to be professional and to show commitment have gone.'[3]

'Trusted to be professional.' A significant phrase. It is because trust has been eroded by the long running conflict between central Government and the teaching unions that as a nation we are far from realising the ideal of having our schools staffed by the true professionals that children deserve.

Notes and references

1 An interesting attempt to square a verbal circle. What does this paragraph actually mean? When does voluntary equal compulsory?
2 Too often we who teach view 'our class' as the limit of our personal responsibility. A school is not a series of individual units but an entity.
3 Quoted from *The Independent* p 1, 21 April, 1987

5 The training of teachers

The methods which a society employs to train its teachers reflect and comment upon the values with which that society is predominately concerned. Following upon the Revolution in the USSR, for example, there was a great need to promote basic literacy and numeracy. Given that narrow aim, the task of the teachers who implemented what was essentially an initial learning programme was tightly prescribed. The primary goal was clear and unequivocal – teach literacy. To achieve this effectively and on a large scale the teaching force would have to concentrate upon the narrow limits which had been set. The young men and women who were suitable for this important work would obviously need to be educated to a level above that of their prospective students. They need not, however, be academic high fliers. By laying down tight guidelines and clear methods of instruction the state could more easily monitor success and at the same time ensure that doctrines and ideas which the party felt to be unacceptable could be excluded from the school curriculum.

A visit to any Eastern European nation will confirm that this approach, more subtly applied, continues. A quotation from a recently published Soviet document makes the position clear.

A curriculum is a state document establishing the subjects which are to be studied at a school of a particular type, their distribution by grades (years) and the number of academic hours per week and per year given to each subject. Syllabuses define the amount and content of knowledge and skill in each subject and lay down their distribution throughout the years that the young person spends at school. Syllabuses are compiled by scholars and methods experts. Standard curriculum and the syllabuses which stem from them are approved by the Ministry of Education.

The task of the institutions which prepare young people to become teachers within the schools is equally clear. The state document defines its expectations of teachers. As a consequence of this, teacher trainers occupy a crucial role, that of developing in students the skills necessary to deliver a centrally defined curriculum package by grade, hour, week and year.

The system is largely self-perpetuating. Children are prepared from the earliest years to move through a tightly controlled educational system. Some, on leaving school, move into teacher training where they are taught how to become the operators of the system of which they themselves are the products.

It is not necessary to draw only upon Eastern Europe for examples of a system of education which is centralised at almost every level below that of research work for higher degrees. In Sweden, a country which prides itself in the freedom of thought and action which it allows its citizens, education from elementary school to college and university is defined and controlled through state boards. As in Yugoslavia or Bulgaria the task of the school is clearly defined. Freedoms there are, but in encouraging a liberal approach to the national work plan which all teachers follow, freedom to ignore the work plan entirely has not been ceded by the state.

In the Swedish system[1] teachers are prepared to work with children within particular grades (1 to 3: 4 to 6: 7 to 9: gymnasium or high school). Teacher training consists of showing students how to deliver the curriculum they will find in schools. Since all the schools follow the same teaching plan and since the content of the programme followed by children in the early years is less demanding academically than that followed by adolescents, it is easy to argue that teachers in the lower grades require less training.

The tightness of the system, even when liberally interpreted, has the effect of restricting experiment. The intellectually gifted find themselves teaching older children; the educationally radical look outside schools for ways of implementing their ideas. There is one other side effect. The salary of the teachers is determined by grade. Teachers in grades 1 to 3 receive a lower salary than those in 4 to 6 (who in turn are paid less than those in grades 7 to 9). The consequence of this weighting is that young children are rarely taught by men. This does little to enhance the status of the woman teacher and nothing towards meeting an important educational need of young people – that of relating to both men and women in the early years of childhood.

Centralised systems of education are organised on a system of 'top-down management'. The power holder (the State, through the Ministry of Education) lays down guidelines. The teaching force then has the task of meeting the criteria established by these guidelines. These criteria are usually formally defined, eg all children of 12 will study the 17th century: the Counter Reformation. It is rare that the 'benchmarks' (the term for criteria used in the popular press) will be as innocuous as those suggested by our politicians.[2] If they are bland, they will be largely ignored. If they are tightly prescribed they will produce an arid conformity in our schools, classrooms and teacher training institutions.

I have chosen this somewhat tangential approach to teacher training in England and Wales because criteria has become one of the central issues of the current educational debate.

For most of the past 100 years our teacher education has been based in specialist colleges. In the 1840s, 1850s and 1860s these colleges were invariably church foundations in which would-be teachers were trained for work in church schools. It was a pattern that the passing of the 1870 Education Act did little to change. Those aspiring to teach the 'labouring class' would be required to show evidence of academic ability a little above the level of those they taught. They would also require some knowledge of educational method.

The dilemma of how to train teachers, which this recipe poses, remains today. The extension of teacher training to three years in the 1960s, which gave students the opportunity of achieving a Bachelors degree in Education (B Ed) in the fourth did little to alter the shape of teacher training. Even when all students were required to read for a degree and the certificate course was phased out, the debate – how much of a teacher's training should be practical and school based, how much purely academic – continued. If the B Ed was a degree which enjoyed the status of all other first degrees, then it must be *and be seen to be* academically respectable. (ie be measurable in all those ways which academics have devised to evaluate their activities). A B Ed student must, therefore, undertake an academic study as part of his/her training (just as the certificated teacher had to do in the 1920s). This academic study was seen as a means of extending, developing and enriching the student's mind and, in as much as it fulfilled this function, had much to commend it. Educational theory and methodology could also become part of this academic enrichment – as could such things as sociology and applied psychology.

It is comparatively easy to expand the academic frontiers of education even further, taking more and more academically respectable (and measurable) elements into the course. But it is much more difficult to justify *on academic terms* an expansion of what I will call 'educational exposure'; the development, through extensive first-hand experience, of an understanding of what being a teacher involves, of the demands it makes upon those who teach for month after month, of the stresses and strains (as well as the joys) of the classroom.

As a past member of several panels of the CNAA[3] (and as a Council Member) I have listened to many discussions about initial teacher training courses planned by polytechnics and colleges. In the great majority of them, the point at issue (whether a course should be given approval or whether approval was withheld) invariably centred upon the balance it achieved between 'academic rigour' and 'professional' skills.

Many of the courses presented were thoroughly and lovingly prepared by lecturers from the polytechnics who fought hard at meetings with the officers of the CNAA and its panels to ensure that the school-centred elements in their courses were given due emphasis. All too often, however, the need for academic respectability meant that the amount of time allocated in such courses to school based work was reduced. 'Academic respectability' prevailed and courses which might have begun to address the key question – what skills and expertise are crucial to the art of teaching and how can these best be learned and applied? – were never developed.

The failure, however, was never total. There remained in the polytechnics (as there had been in the former teacher training colleges) lecturers who, having experience of teaching in primary schools, acknowledged the importance of approaching teacher education in a broader, more holistic way. Young children, they argued, are wide ranging in their interests and enthusiasms. They drink in experience, reflecting and commenting upon their discoveries in words, spoken and written, in paint, dance, drama and model making. They do not fit their newly found knowledge into the neat compartments so beloved by academics. This curiosity about the world and the way in which children's understanding of that world is coloured and influenced by their individual experiences are characteristic of all young children.

If understanding the way children think, how they respond to experience and how adults can identify the messages which children give through their behaviour, are central to the teacher's art, then initial teacher training should offer more than lip service to classroom experience. Insights into child development do not only come from books. Theory needs to be grounded in practice.

The English primary school (which at its best has provided a model for educationalists across the world) has one unique characteristic. It has been generalist rather than specific, its programme being based upon each child's interests and abilities (rather than upon an external authority's projection of what they ought to be). The teacher servicing this kind of classroom has also been a generalist, seeing his/her task in terms of need-meeting rather than simple goal setting. Goals will, of course, be set. But they will be individual goals, not collective ones. The child of seven who can read fluently will not be held back so that an identical level of attainment can be achieved by all: the slow learner will not become the victim of a system which challenges him to achieve a goal which is unattainable.

If teacher training is about preparing young men and women to work sensitively to children's needs, and to provide a work force of newly trained teachers who are able to fit into schools effectively, the way in which initial teacher education is developing deserves careful reappraisal.

This is not to say that the 'generalists' (with whom I would number myself) are sceptical of scholarly writing and research. Teacher education, as Dr William Taylor,[4] has pointed out, is 'Janus faced'. It looks two ways

> into the classroom and the school with demands for relevance, practicality, competence, technique . . . Yet its very two headedness should not encourage us to eschew effective practice on the grounds that theory and ideology are intellectually more satisfying.

At the moment the generalists are losing ground. Those who prepare courses of initial teaching training must (in addition to meeting conditions laid down by the CNAA) also satisfy the requirements of the Government's Advisory Committee on the Supply and Education of Teachers (CATE). This committee, like the CNAA, gives the approval necessary before a course can be funded (and thereby receive students). Its present role is to examine course structure and ensure that each approved B Ed course contains defined basic elements – for example, that 100 hours be devoted to mathematics, a further 100 to English language and defined hours for the student's own subject specialism.

Concentration upon specific specialisms during initial training dovetails neatly into a recommendation (which has been made by successive Secretaries of State and supported by members of HM Inspectorate) that each primary school should be staffed by teachers whose individual academic strengths represent principal subject areas (eg language, mathematics, creative arts, environmental studies, science and technology). These specialists or 'consultants' are not intended to teach only their own subject. They will work as generalists too. However as subject specialists they will be able to offer older primary school children 'the sort of organisation that they will meet in the secondary school'. This was Kenneth Baker's observation. It prompts me to wonder why secondary school organisation (not conspicuously successful) should be moved into our primary schools.

It is not within the scope of this chapter to reflect upon how such a combined change (in teacher training and school organisation) might affect the quality and style of young children's learning. Suffice it to say that it is likely to be difficult – if not impossible – for each school to maintain a balance of consultants. Does one appoint a poor teacher who is a mathematics specialist to a staff rather than an excellent teacher who happens to be a historian but who enjoys teaching mathematics? Is an organisation which is common to secondary schools (subject-based teaching) necessarily appropriate for younger children? In responding to such criticism, Jim Rose, Chief Inspector for Primary Education, suggested that both the specialist and generalist class teacher have a part to play. 'There needs to be a judicious mixture of both forms of organisation to make the best use of the talents of the teachers.'

Teacher training can also be undertaken at university departments of education. Here, students who have already graduated, can become qualified teachers by taking a year's course which leads to the award of PGCE.[5] For these students discussion on specialism within the course structure does not apply. Their degree is evidence of their academic ability in a particular subject area. Nevertheless it is pertinent to observe that while academic studies at college and polytechnics are presented as being important because they enrich the student, the subjects which are acceptable for entry to a primary PGCE course are clearly defined. A graduate in psychology, archaeology or Oriental studies is not able to take a PGCE Primary course on the grounds (I assume) that such specialisms are inappropriate to the primary school setting. The division (between those graduates who may undertake training and those who because of the discipline of their first degrees may not) is arbitrary and illogical.

Quality of mind, response to children and understanding of young people's needs is what is needed of our primary school teachers. Few graduates in English use their 'academic' knowledge of Restoration Comedy in their day to day work in the reception class. Their degree reflects their interest and comments upon their specific abilities. The training which is offered by PGCE courses (whether at polytechnic or university) should be devoted to giving graduates some understanding of the nature and needs of the children with whom they are to work.

One could question whether in the year which is allowed to them, tutors responsible for PGCE students can hope to fulfil the demands placed upon them. In one short year class organisation and management, teaching skills, methodology (which will include those many initial strategies appropriate to the teaching of reading and early mathematics) must be mastered. The place of the Arts, drama, music, painting, must be touched upon; the education system, its organisation and history, explained and clarified.

And yet, if my experience is typical, I found the majority of PGCE students responsive to the demands such an intense course made upon them. They were able to concentrate upon the task of becoming a teacher. The demands placed upon them by academic subjects could be put on one side, they could devote their minds with urgency to the mastery of new skills and knowledge.

This separation of personal and academic studies from classroom-based activities is reflected in the courses which are offered. If, for example, the bulk of the academic element is contained in the first two years of a course, then the second two can be devoted to developing teaching strategies. A common alternative is the spread of 'academic' and school elements throughout the four years. When this happens it is more likely that the two strands mix indifferently.

The sorry thing about teacher training is that it remains within such a restricting framework. Students spend more years on initial training courses than they have ever done. And to what end? The methods employed – lecture, seminar, essay, school practice, school visit, methodology in theory and practice – remain as they were when I was trained. They may be packaged slightly differently but they are based upon the same unspoken tradition that underpinned my own short years at college. Instruction of the would-be teacher takes place in academic institutions far removed from the reality of the children's world.

This is compounded by a second problem. Young people who undertake teacher training are representative of a small proportion of the school population – the academically successful. So often they bring to their training elements drawn from their own experience of school. They, the academically gifted, responded to ideas which their teachers (themselves academic) offered. They succeeded because they were able (and willing) to play the examination game. I am convinced that what is needed in initial teacher education is not just to instil respect for a particular form of academic learning. There must also be an attempt to give students insight into perceptions of school held by children and their parents.

Children live in a sub-culture of their own. For a considerable minority of children school has little relevance. This sad state of affairs may be attributed to feckless parents or to a society which projects its standards and values in such an ambivalent way. Apportioning of blame (to home, social conditions, indifferent teaching) will not resolve the situation or prevent tomorrow's schools becoming a battleground littered with the emotional corpses of children and teachers.

The young teacher who goes from success at school to success at college and university (like his/her Swedish or Russian counterpart) is likely to take back into school as a teacher the assumptions which underpinned this personal success. Some of the children such teachers will meet will have motives and aspirations similar to their own. Many will not. Attitudes to school, the significance of the curriculum, perceptions of the nature of society . . . are learned early[6] and impossible to reshape in classrooms which are run by teachers who are unaware that such tensions exist.

Of the initiatives which have been undertaken to enable would-be teachers to better understand the nature of children, that pioneered by Frank Coles (and latterly by Roger Tingle) at the Urban Studies Centre, Poplar, East London, is perhaps one of the most significant.

The programme, which began in the early 1970s, aimed at helping students to reassess their own assumptions by giving them first-hand experience of the life and social conditions in which many children grow and develop. For this reason the centre was placed in a deprived area of East London. Students are invited to undertake a programme combining, concurrently, the traditional teaching practice with a social work placement. The latter might be in a playgroup, a hostel for severely handicapped children, a second language centre for immigrant women, an intermediate treatment centre, or a community education shop.

During this dual placement students meet children and

their parents in the traditional setting of school and in the less structured setting provided by a youth club or city farm. Social workers as well as lecturers in education contribute to the course input. Living within a decaying urban community in which traditional values have been eroded, the students come to see, perhaps for the first time, the relationship between school and the community. Children go to the former for six hours a day to follow an educational programme, which in some aspects is quite unrelated to their culture; they live in the latter, their world shaped by their parents. The unspoken law of street and playground, the economic and social pressures of decay (and the disenchantment which it brings), often offer a stark contrast to the views and values presented to them in school.

That such a programme was adopted and continues to expand is a reflection both of the dedication of the staff and of the need which it meets.[7] By immersing students within the community and employing professionals from other disciplines to present insights which are different from, though complementary to, those of teacher trainers, the Centre encourages students to question the very basis on which they plan their teaching programme. What do these children need of me? How relevant is this topic I plan to teach? Can I present the Norman Invasion of 1066 to this group of Bengali children? Even if I think I can present it, should I do so? Put simply, the Urban Studies Centre seeks to equip students to understand children and to sharpen their insight. It is impossible to teach children as though each fits a neatly turned theory. To teach effectively (whether it be in the backstreets of Birmingham, in the gentility of Bath or the quietness of Beaumaris) the teacher must come to appreciate and understand the lifestyle of the children in his or her care. What is important is that each student is made aware of the chasm which separates the comfortable assumptions we make as teachers and the reality of the world beyond the school walls. The divide occurs in all areas, with the rich and the affluent as well as the seedy and derelict.

There is another gulf to be bridged. This is the division

between those who teach in teacher training institutions and the schools themselves. There has always been criticism, much of it unjust, that lecturers in colleges and polytechnics fail to keep in touch with school-based initiatives and developments and that college programmes are all too often divorced from the real world of school.

The Roehampton Institute in Surrey consists of four component colleges (Digby Stuart, Froebel, Southlands, Whitelands). The former Dean of the Institute, Dr Marten Shipman, believed that it was essential for schools and teacher training institutions to play a shared role in the development of students. At Roehampton he achieved this by encouraging staff from the college to spend time working in schools, at the same time offering experienced teachers and headteachers the opportunity to lead courses within the Institute. By bringing immediate experience of the classroom into college courses, perceptions within college about the work of schools were heightened. By taking the college, through its tutors, into schools, academic insights were offered informally to school staff. In 1985–86, for example, Roehampton Institute engaged a headteacher to work with a college for six hours a week and ten other teachers for three hours a week.[8] The commitment in every case was for two academic years.

The Roehampton experiment has much to commend it. It has strengthened links between school and college, it encourages dialogue, it gives opportunity to classroom teachers to develop new skills and to take on new responsibilities. This is particularly important at a time when there is little mobility in the education service.

When I visited Roehampton to prepare an article for the *Times Educational Supplement*, Dr Shipman expressed his hopes that the scheme would 'lead to an initial preparation for teaching that blends theory and practice in courses that are coherent and intellectually stretching'. It depends for success upon the goodwill and support of the LEAs and the schools. To establish firm links, tutors are allocated to groups of schools so that staff come to know their tutor well.

The schools help us. We help the schools. Ideally as we get more and more teachers involved in the work we do, initial training will be based even more firmly upon school experience. The professional development of future teachers could then take place in the classroom.

The initiatives at the Urban Studies Centre and at Roehampton indicate something which faces those responsible for the training of primary school teachers. Both initiatives seek to add a more practical element to teacher training. Both point to the need to give students experiences which will give life to the theoretical elements which are also essential parts of their course.

In all educational practice lies a vision of the future. The future of our primary schools is rooted in the institutions which train our teachers. Fashions in education will come and go, politicians, local and national, will peddle their transitory wares, but the long-term effectiveness of our schools will depend ultimately upon there being sufficient teachers of quality to work in the nation's classrooms.

It is unlikely that narrow initiatives (like criteria targeting based upon statistical projections of likely future needs) will provide schools with the workforce which is required. Breaking the traditional mould of teacher training is not going to be easy. And yet that is what is needed.

It is worth recalling that some of the most effective teachers in England in the 1950s and 1960s were not conventionally trained. They came from the armed forces, from war work, from factory, farm, workshop and office. Then, academic credibility established, they undertook an intensive one year course.

I would not suggest that a return to such a programme is either necessary or appropriate. Nevertheless the emergency training scheme served to show that the maturity and work experience gained outside the classroom could contribute a great deal to the life and work of our schools, enriching them in both classroom and staffroom.

Notes and references

1 Swedish children enter elementary school at 7 (Grade 1) and leave at 16 (end of Grade 9). Currently (1987) the Swedish Government is exploring the possibility of allowing children to enter school at 6 and of training teachers to teach across grades 1–7 and 3–9.

2 One of Kenneth Baker's suggested benchmarks is that all 11 year olds will have read *Animal Farm*. Dr Rhodes Boyson has also remarked that the ability to read a Dickens novel and a play by Shakespeare could be used, at the secondary level, as an indicator of academic competence.

3 The Council for National Academic Awards validates degrees, certificates and diplomas offered by polytechnics and similar institutions of higher education. It operates through a range of panels and committees, which are in turn responsible to its governing council.

4 Dr Taylor is currently Vice Chancellor of Hull University and Chairman of the Advisory Committee on the Supply and Education of Teachers (CATE).

5 Postgraduate Certificate in Education.

6 A young mother speaking on BBC radio about the confrontation between police and strikers in Wapping observed 'Whenever I took my pushchair past the pickets my three-year-old son raised his fist towards the printing works and shouted "Scab!".'

7 Students attend the centre from a group of Anglican colleges. Participating colleges link their courses to the programme offered by the Centre.

8 For evening employment the teachers receive payment from the Institute. If employment is in school time, the LEA is compensated. The Institute therefore indirectly meets the salary of the replacement teacher.

6 The school: educational plant and social centre

The history of education is littered with discarded phrases, phrases which were once fashionable and seemed to encapsulate the spirit of a Utopia soon to be born. Some of these phrases relate to a particular teaching style (the project approach, the integrated day); some refer to organisation ('all-through' comprehensives) and some to architecture (open plan with resource areas). More significant than these are the phrases which imply that teachers have a responsibility which extends beyond the school gates.

The idea of community schools is not a new one. Village colleges were successfully established in Cambridgeshire in the 1920s and 1930s. (Indeed they continue to flourish.) These colleges were built as an educational resource, meeting the needs of children during the school day and providing space (and sometimes staff) at other times for adult clubs and classes.

When such a programme develops the school inevitably becomes more open to the community. Adults, many of them without children of their own, go into schools for their classes. Having received the unspoken messages which every corner gives (the condition of the toilets, the way books in the library are presented, the displays along corridors and in classrooms, the amount of litter around the building, the beauty or devastation of the flower beds, the graffiti on the walls) judgements are made about school and schooling.

Such judgements may be ill-informed, they may not take into account the social stresses within the area, they may simply feed prejudices already held. Nevertheless, once a school opens its gates to a broader public than the one it has been designed to serve, its staff can no longer work in an educational laager, isolated from the outside world.

Community education, which may have been encouraged by the homely style for school building adopted by architects after the Second World War, became the 'buzz' phrase of the 1960s. The school 'plant' began to be seen not just as a resource which could be used for adult education or the occasional PTA dance and parents' meeting. Instead it came to be regarded as a base from which the school could reach out into the community.

There were a number of reasons for this subtle change. The social and economic upheavals which stemmed from the war were profound. The pattern of family life changed. The simultaneous emergence of the nuclear family and housing developments which swept away streets and replaced them with tower blocks, contributed to an erosion (and even total destruction) of many communities. Although the 'Coronation Streets' of pre-war Britain may have lacked many of the amenities we now take for granted, at least they gave a sense of continuity in community to the people living in them – a sense which was buried in the concrete of municipal improvement.

This slow disappearance of long established communities was accompanied by a collectivisation of professionals who had once served them. The family doctor was replaced by the much more impersonal group practice. The GP who had for generations been regarded as much as a family advisor as a curer of disease, became a thing of the past. To talk to a doctor one was first required to outmanoeuvre the often formidable receptionist. Even then any appointment granted would rarely be immediate.

Similarly the church was turning increasingly to group ministries. The black cassocked priest was a common sight in the streets of my South London childhood. Regular worshippers may have been as sparse then as they are today but he was a person to whom one turned in times of trouble, just as he was called on at times of family celebration. At the very least he was known and accessible.

These changes, together with a greater mobility in the workforce made possible by an expansion of car ownership, created a vacuum. At times of sudden and unexpected crises there was no identifiable person to whom young (and often inexperienced) parents could easily turn. Often they lived in an impersonal tower block some distance from their immediate relatives. The focal point of the community was the super-market or the Bingo Hall rather than the church. The family doctor was a name on a card rather than a face to be recognised in the street. All of these changes were happening at a time when the rapid expansion of television was encouraging even greater isolation. The TV set was beginning to fulfill the roles of third parent, surrogate husband, and surrogate wife.

Against such a background it is easy to understand how the school became the personal face of the welfare state. For many years teachers had occupied a somewhat ambiguous position. They had been expected to supervise school meals, to distribute milk, to be responsible for children at lunch times. For a number of years after the war they were also expected to administer to their classes a daily dose of cod liver oil tablets and a spoonful of malt. Teachers also collected national savings, organised and staffed country holidays for needy children, alerted the school nurse when scabies or head lice appeared, and kept a watchful eye for children who might be suffering from difficulties in sight and hearing. The Social Services also expected co-operation from school, for teachers, in daily close contact with children, were admirably placed to read the tell-tale signs of brutal, cruel or inadequate parenting.

The gradual expansion of the teacher's role from presenter of information to carer was as accidental as it was logical. A child who came to school at the age of five dirty and smelling of urine would never be able to benefit from the experience of school if, as a consequence, she were shunned and rejected by her classmates. A nine year old whose father had just left the family home would be unlikely to be able to concentrate upon mathematics or science if he were beset with worries about his mother. Perhaps the greatest contribution which our primary schools have made to education since the war has been to focus attention upon the child as a whole, unique human being. Intellectual needs will have to be met, but the meeting of these needs may not be possible until other needs – physical, emotional and social – are first satisfied. Put another way, a child will learn most effectively when there is harmony. To teach effectively teachers must therefore be aware of facets of the child's life which are contributing to tension and disquiet.

Improved communication about children and the problems which they faced outside school was not simply a consequence of a rapidly changing society. It was also a reflection of a growing awareness on the part of teachers that learning in school would be more effective if parents were helped to understand what they, the teachers, were seeking to achieve. In other words the impetus which took the community into school and the school into the community came from two different directions. When parents needed someone outside the family with whom to share a problem, the school (usually through the head teacher) provided 'the human face'. Teachers, though in some cases suspicious that these new demands were turning them into social workers, realised that this role brought them benefits. A school which is seen to be supporting its clients is much more likely to be supported in turn, by the community it is there to serve.

The growing dialogue between teacher and parents received favourable comment in the Plowden Report. Following upon publication of the Report many interesting experiments in school-home co-operation were undertaken. In some schools, rooms were provided for parents. Often they were simply meeting places where young mothers could chat and share problems. Sometimes these informal meetings led parents to form a task force to help meet a particular school need – covering library books, repairing and repainting of toys, making simple equipment or assisting teachers with classroom chores.

In some schools the involvement went even further. In one South West London School (opened in 1968) a special workshop-club was provided in which parents could meet regularly after school (from 5 to 7 pm) to take part in a wide range of shared activities such as model making and the arts.

In the school for which I was responsible (which also opened in 1968) parents were encouraged to share their particular skills and knowledge with teachers and children. This led to the establishment of after-school clubs for children of junior age, staffed by a team of teachers and parents and to the provision of an activities programme for under-tens in the summer holiday, organised through the Parent-Teacher Association.

Such a commitment, which was not untypical, was demanding of teachers and parents. Yet the schools in which this coming together of parent and teacher in the service of children occurred had immense benefits. Parents, often isolated and often with a view of children based only upon their experience of their own offspring, began to be able to set their child and his/her behaviour within a much broader context. Parents saw *and began to understand* the difficulties which teachers faced and became more sympathetic and supportive.

There were many other benefits. Children of pre-school age came into school with their mothers and fathers. They met teachers and other children. The tensions associated with starting school could begin to be dissolved long before that anxiously awaited first day, a day which often causes more anguish to parents than it does to their children.

In areas where a first generation immigrant community was being established, the invitation into schools was often received with some apprehension and not a little disbelief. Even now, in the late 1980s, schools continue to attempt to bridge the cultural gap which exists between races. A group of Bengali mothers who attend their children's primary school in

East London to be helped towards an understanding of English language and the mysteries of local government administration might appear to be making an insignificant contribution to their children's educational well being. Yet I would maintain that any structure, however informal, which develops and strengthens parental understanding of the *process* of education (ie the way young children learn) as well as the *product* (ie the measured achievement) is to be commended.

The coming together of teacher and parent on an informal basis had the effect of encouraging parents to turn to teachers for advice. Requests for help tend to centre upon children within the family but when financial or emotional disaster strikes the advice sought centres upon much more fundamental questions than progress in literacy or computation. Indeed it could be argued that a family crisis (for example the suicide of a father) is bound to have a long term effect upon the child. How easy is it to show concern for school work when a beloved father takes you to school in the morning and kills himself by midday? If one parent can do such a thing, can a child really accept that his mother will not disappear with equal suddenness tomorrow?

Reacting to such problems (and the suicide mentioned above was one of three encountered in my period of headship) has proved to be a heavy additional burden to many teachers. At a very early stage in my career I learned that a sympathetic response on my part to the child's needs within the family setting made my work as a classroom teacher considerably easier. I also noticed that in those schools in which I worked where the head, as a matter of policy, distanced himself from parents, my understanding of the children with whom I worked was less complete. In schools where headteachers were responsive, the information which was passed to me often provided vital insights into a child's difficulties.

On becoming a head I was determined to try to give parents the opportunity to talk freely and frankly about their children and their children's needs. Inexperienced as I was in counselling, I nevertheless felt it essential that the school should offer itself as a support agency through which parents could find their way into the numerous services provided by the state, by the local authority and by voluntary organisations.

To this end, and with the support of the local authority, I established a support group for parents. It consisted of a team of people who met on a regular basis and who made themselves available to share their expertise with parents. The group was made up of an educational psychologist, a psychiatric social worker, an educational welfare worker and myself. The problems presented ranged from sexual problems within marriage to alcoholism, suicide, attempted suicide, indecent assault upon a child, physical violence between husband and wife, family breakdown, learning and behavioural problems of children (eg sibling rivalry, stealing, incendiarism), terminal illness within the family and bereavement.

The purpose of the group was not to solve the problem but to share it. In sharing, each 'specialist' was able to suggest ways in which ongoing professional help could be obtained. The fact that school was the place at which the group met was important. Visiting a school is so much easier than sitting exposed in the waiting room of a specialist institution. To the discussions (when appropriate for them to do so) came the classteacher, the school nurse, the social worker who knew the family, the family priest. In my first ten years of headship over 100 families used the service which the school provided, often returning to share with the group the progress which had been made and to comment on the ways in which their children had responded to the advice they had been given.

This sharing of skills from a range of disciplines cannot be anything but beneficial to children and their parents. Teachers do not have exclusive knowledge. They can bring, through their training and experience, particular and specified ways of looking at a child's problem. What is becoming increasingly obvious is that in a society growing ever more stressful and complex, we cannot hope to educate children as though they were immune to the social, economic and emotional stresses which their parents have to bear. Although school *has* an important part to play in a young child's total development, the tensions of life beyond the classroom are likely to be the ones which determine educational failure or educational success.

I am aware that this viewpoint is a personal one, and is by no means accepted by all teachers. Nevertheless, in recent years we have been moving, albeit slowly and hesitantly, towards the view that the primary school should regard itself as one element in a united national service to children. To share skills and expertise is not to dilute 'professionalism', but to enhance it. To proclaim that education is part of a caring social service is not to diminish the part which the education plays, but to enrich and deepen it.

It is for this reason that I regard the industrial action which swept through schools in the mid-1980s with regret. It seems to me to indicate a failure on the part of the union activists to understand that by 'withdrawing good will', the state education service has lost much of the respect so painstakingly built up by successive generations of teachers. The acceptance of a contract which sets out detailed conditions of service, hours worked and parents met is unlikely to provide the flexibility that is required for schools to respond quickly, humanely and sympathetically to family needs. In my opinion it is this flexibility which has given English primary education its unique quality. In the countries in which I have worked where tight regulations prescribe the teachers' day, the opportunity for intelligent freedom of action is all too often curtailed and responses to the problems which children present are all too often determined by the paragraph and footnote of a rule book.

Children and their parents are human. Being human the problems they present are unique, the ways of responding to them infinite. The particular quality of the English primary school has been the way in which its teachers have been able to respond to the individual child on a personal, almost intuitive, basis. I do not believe that a contract which clarifies hours worked or tasks to be done will prevent teachers from caring, but it may make it rather more difficult to implement school-based initiatives.

The view that the teacher should be seen as a key worker within a caring social network has been criticised on a number of grounds. Teachers, we are told, are ill equipped to undertake such work. Those responsible for initial teacher training cannot hope to find time or personnel for the additional input which would be required. Personally I am convinced that unless initiatives like that undertaken by the Urban Studies Centre (see page 95) are adopted, we will continue to train teachers who, though they have impeccable paper qualifications, lack the real life experience which will give credibility to the certificates, degrees and diplomas they have so earnestly won.

There are those, too, who have attacked the idea of an expanded role for teachers on much narrower grounds. 'Teachers are paid to teach. The school in which they work is a building especially designed for teaching'. To take this view is to diminish teaching, presenting it as a form of fact processing, ignoring in the process the holistic view of the child within the family unit.

The clash between Government and teaching unions certainly made it more difficult to extend the teacher's role. And yet, what is required, if teachers are ever to enjoy the prestige of true professionals, is to encourage them to reach out into the society they are there to serve, rather than for them to retreat behind their school walls.

Hopefully, sometime in the future, it will be possible to create community schools from which a new breed of professional will emerge. These social-work teachers may have a school base; certainly they would have flexible hours in order that they could meet the needs of young people during times when schools were closed (early evenings, long holidays). They may relate to one institution (a primary school) or to several (linking a number of primary schools to the neighbourhood secondary school), they may relate to primary age children within a community centre or youth club, they may simply serve as a bridge between local pre-school playgroups and the schools which the pre-school children will eventually attend. Their everyday work would bring them into touch with a wide range of people – parents, grandparents, professionals working in other disciplines, voluntary agencies. They would be available to share expertise, offer advice and provide an informed focus for locally based educational advance.

This shift of emphasis, the seeds of which were sown in the 1960s and 1970s, would root teachers much more firmly in the communities they serve. Teachers involved in such work could not but become aware of broad local issues as well as the hopes, fears and anxieties of individual families. In devoting a small proportion of a local teaching force to this wider brief, one significant benefit is likely to result. Teachers will begin to learn from the consumer, rather than from the articulate politician, the real aspirations of the local community. As I found when I took the time to listen to parents and *hear what they said*, the views advanced did not always fit the latest fashion or an approved passage in a book on sociology. Neither did they always reflect forward looking views on education. But as I quickly discovered, if any real progress is to be made even the most reactionary views need to be listened to and respected. Counter them we must, for the resulting dialogue offers both parties the opportunity to grasp and hopefully come to understand contrasting viewpoints.

The contemporary primary school, because of its small size and the daily contact which it has with parents, is in a unique position to offer a comprehensive educational/social service. It can provide a safety net for children in danger as well as for those who have socially or emotionally lost their way.

To do so effectively requires a commitment from the teaching force – from headteacher to probationer. Unfortunately this is a commitment which is unlikely to be supported by higher pay or additional allowances. To a large extent, however, it's what working in an education service is all about – caring for today's young people in order that they will be more able to cope with the complexities of a society teachers and parents will never live to see.

7 Children with special needs

Special schools. The very phrase implies exclusion, segregation, a particular approach to learning and teaching. The 1944 Education Act made local education authorities responsible for providing education for all children according to their 'needs, aptitudes and abilities'. The act, therefore, required that LEAs provide schools which would meet the needs of *all* children including those who were suffering from serious physical or mental disabilities. The categories of handicap which were listed as requiring special provision were: blind, partially sighted, deaf, partially deaf, delicate/diabetic, educationally subnormal, epileptic, maladjusted, physically handicapped and children with special defects. Whilst it was intended that children with minor handicaps would be able to attend mainstream schools, the act required that the blind, deaf, epileptic, physically handicapped and aphasic children must be educated in special schools.

For the 2% of children who were 'ascertained' as needing special education the 1950s and 1960s were years of isolation. Special schools existed in all local authorities but rarely were the children who attended given the opportunity to share everyday experiences with their more fortunate contemporaries.

The 1970s were marked by a steady but subtle change. Medical advances resulted in educationalists, physicians and psychologists becoming aware that the classifications of handicap which were being used failed to take into account the complexity of individual disability. This was accompanied by the realisation that to isolate handicapped children from their contemporaries was to harm both groups. The handicapped child, who would eventually have to move into society, would be ill-equipped to face that society's tensions and realities whilst the 'normal' child would have had no experience, during the impressionable and formative years, of relating to the disabled. The movement towards integration (with its social, moral, philosophical and educational overtones) was to be found in many countries and was part of an international concern for the place which the handicapped occupied in Western society.

When attention was given to individual children it became clear that a far more effective way of viewing the disabled was not in terms of *handicap* but in terms of personal *need*. In other words, there is no sharp divide between a child who is 'handicapped' and a child who is 'normal'. To some extent both will have a similar range of needs but each will occupy a different place within this range.

In the summer of 1974 a committee chaired by Mary Warnock was established to consider how to make educational provision for the handicapped more effective. The committee reported in May 1978, in a document of some 400 pages containing 224 recommendations. In it the committee emphasised the uniqueness of each child, stressing that the goals of education were

> to enlarge a child's knowledge, experience and understanding, develop his awareness of moral values and to enable him to become 'an active' and 'responsible' participant in society . . . capable of achieving as much independence as possible.

The report went on to point out that these goals were the same for all children, although some children will realise them (all or in part) at a much slower pace than others. Thus all children, whether suffering from disability or not, have similar needs. These needs should be seen as a reason for unifying rather than for dividing educational provision. If need rather than a particular handicap is made the measure against which provision shall be made, the needs of each child must be clearly identified and regularly reviewed and realised.

This analysis led to three key recommendations:

1 The provision of special education must be measured against its effectiveness in meeting the needs of the handicapped child.

2 Wherever appropriate, children with special educational needs should be integrated into the community. (In an educational context this meant 'mainstream' primary and secondary schools.)

3 To ensure that this was accomplished as effectively as possible there should be positive discrimination in favour of those who have special needs.

After much public discussion and debate, the principles of the Warnock report were enshrined in an Act of Parliament (Education Act 1981), its main provisions being implemented on 1 April 1983.

The workings of the Act require that every child with special needs be individually assessed to determine whether

a child's needs are such as to require provision additional to or otherwise different from the facilities and resources generally available in ordinary schools in the area under normal arrangements.

The formal assessment, which involves reports on each child from teachers, psychologists, doctors and perhaps social workers, and requires a degree of parental co-operation, is time-consuming, but undoubtedly necessary.

The assessment, against which the parent can appeal, seeks to identify a child's specific needs and is then used as the basis for eventual school placement. The recommendation following upon an assessment might result in a child with a hearing disability being placed in a local primary school rather than in a special unit for children who are deaf or partially hearing. The staff of the receiving primary school would be alerted to the child's particular needs. At the same time the teacher who takes the child into his/her class would be supported by regular visits from an experienced teacher of the deaf.

Not all children with special needs are integrated within mainstream schools. Some, the most severely handicapped, continue to have their needs met in schools designed to cater for their degree of disability.

In theory the approach is admirable. In practice – and I write from experience – the Act has been under-resourced. Identifying the educational needs of a handicapped child falls within the province of an experienced teacher. But if the child is a paraplegic spina-bifida victim, for example, the receiving teacher should surely expect to receive additional training to equip him/her to cope with the physical implications of the condition. Unfortunately this does not always happen and when it does there is often insufficient time given to such training.

Lack of support for mainstream teachers is not only reflected through inadequate training. One special needs child is not necessarily the equivalent of one 'mainstream' child. The level of attention which a special needs child might merit and deserve may not be possible – or the programme which the rest of the class follow may have to be skewed or truncated or adapted for them to be integrated.

An additional difficulty arises when special needs children are taken onto the roll of a primary school before appropriate adaptations have been made to the school building. Toilets often need to be redesigned and re-sited, ramps laid, incinerators and changing beds installed. All too often, in my experience, lack of finance frustrates the good intentions of even the most supportive of local authorities.

Having touched upon the logistical difficulties of implementing the Warnock proposals, I should observe that working with 'special needs' children within a conventional primary school enriches the whole community – children, teachers and parents. To mainstream children it offers the opportunity to live with and work alongside children who are triumphing over pain and crippling disability. It breeds both acceptance and admiration. At the same time the child with special needs is challenged intellectually and socially. A wheelchair is no barrier to success in creative writing, using a computer, painting a picture – or to the development of long-lasting friendships.

The primary school has been called 'the school of all the people'. The vision of the Warnock Report has helped to extend this principle still further. What is needed now is far greater resources, both physical and human, in order that this ideal can be realised.

Warnock, inadequately funded though it may be, serves to indicate real concern for the child who is disabled. The political admission of responsibility is a mark of our collective concern.

We seem to show less awareness, however, for a second group of exceptional children, the 2% who experience learning difficulties because they are too bright. The difficulties they face are just as special as those faced by the emotionally disturbed or the physically handicapped. For gifted children much of the school day can be at the best an irrelevance, at the worst a tedious obstruction to effective learning.

It is not that teachers in our primary schools dislike teaching bright children. It is not that children of high intelligence are somehow debarred from having a rich and satisfying school life. Too often, however, the academic progress of the gifted child is held back by the way classrooms and teaching are organised. The approach to primary education endorsed by the Plowden committee was one in which individual programmes of learning were supported by group work and whole class lessons. This pattern is one which allows each child to learn at his or her own pace. In classrooms where such a pattern exists personal pace and achievement can be taken as the yardstick against which learning is measured. This on-going assessment side-steps dependence upon the concept of 'average'. When a system of individual assessment is implemented, teachers seek regularly and conscientiously to perceive a child's success (be this in reading, in mathematics, or in the slow mastery of a concept in history or science) against the understanding that child showed yesterday, last week or last year. Similarly tomorrow's hopes for the child must be set against the understanding shown today. Just as degrees of handicap must be seen against a continuum of need, so must the learning of individual children.

Learning is not a collective activity. It is something which happens in Fred's head. It is this we must grasp if we are to challenge those who would seek to impose a tight curriculum upon all children. It is immaterial to Fred or Mary or Shaida whether the curriculum is designed by the state, the local authority or the school. Once we begin to build primary education from neat blocks of acceptable and appropriate knowledge, teachers will tend to teach accordingly. Since the knowledge required will be prescribed, the tendency will be (as it has always been in teaching) to present it in such a form as to be acceptable to the average child. The slower children will be disadvantaged because the work offered is too difficult; the more able children will be disadvantaged because the challenge that school should offer them has disappeared.

If I were invited to make a criticism of primary school teachers within an international setting it would be to suggest that our expectation of children's ability is too low. I have yet to visit a country where children are not stereotyped to some extent – by class, social background, race, culture, colour, sex. Children so treated all too quickly respond to their teacher's unspoken assumptions.

The task of teachers is to help the less able master basic skills, to meet the needs of the children of average ability and to encourage and satisfy the needs of the children who are exceptionally able. Gifted children are not peculiar to one ethnic group or to a particular social class. Yet at the moment there is a feeling in many of the schools I visit (both in this country and abroad) that to give attention to the child who is already a 'high flier' is difficult and somehow immoral. 'He learns so quickly' one teacher observed to me 'that I feel unnecessary'. The 'he' in question was about six years old! If we are to succeed as teachers (or parents) we must accept that children may well be brighter than us and blessed with a potential far beyond our own.

This fear of being intellectually inadequate (an unnecessary fear where we, the adults, have so much experience of life to share with the children in our care) is eased by a subconscious desire to help the less able. When this feeling is fostered by a political climate which proclaims egalitarianism and equality for all, the implementation of a school programme for the gifted becomes even more difficult to achieve.

I am not arguing here for a return to streaming or special provision for children with exceptional gifts. What I *am* suggesting is that if education is for all then it must meet all needs. The seven year old who shows outstanding promise when playing the violin, the eight year old who is fascinated with negative numbers, the four year old who can read fluently, the eleven year old who can design computer programmes . . . must have these gifts cherished, not have them dismissed or confined.

For too long as a society we have neglected the potential of our children. The child who has particular gifts has the right to have these developed for the common good of the society he will eventually enter as an adult. It is in our primary schools that potential above the commonplace is likely to be first identified. It is in our primary schools that such potential can be tended or crushed. If it is crushed, then the retreat from state education into the private sector will continue. Even though independent schools are just as neglectful in the courses which are offered to the non-convergent child as are their state counterparts, at least their parents draw comfort from a feeling that, through their cheque books, they are signalling respect for quality and individualism.

Although such 'signals' may be born of snobbism and élitism of the least attractive kind and are often public confirmations of economic privilege, those teachers who have devoted their working lives to the state sector know that the only way of countering, undermining and finally defeating private eduction is by making the local authority schools places where *all* children realise their full potential. That means meeting the needs of the exceptionally gifted as well as those of the physically handicapped and socially deprived.

8 Parents – a changing role

Teachers tend to forget that education is a political activity. School, paid for and sponsored by the state, provides the only effective means of inculcating the values which the state would wish its future citizens to hold. In Eastern block countries the school curriculum is used to confirm a particular view of social and economic organisation; in countries where the Roman Catholic Church enjoys power and influence the school curriculum reflects its dogma and teaching; in nations where the values of social democracy are paramount (like Sweden) all schools follow programmes which confirm the part which men and women must play as responsible, socially conscious citizens.

In Britain the connection between politics and curriculum is less immediately obvious. Nevertheless, as soon as we begin to probe beneath the surface of the contemporary debate, political concerns sometimes seem to outweigh educational ones. As right-wing politicians proclaim that the school curriculum must help children understand Britain's 'place in the world', the virtues of defence or popular capitalism, their left-wing counterparts maintain that schools should concern themselves with issues like the role of the police in contemporary society, homosexuality and the rights of cultural and ethnic minorities.

Political intervention also occurs in a much brasher, more destructive form. When industry seems to be failing, the politically quick-witted can attribute much of the problem to schools and their inability to prepare children adequately for the world of work. Similarly when petty crime increases the lack of school discipline is offered as the principal contributing factor. When there is confrontation on the streets or on the picket line we are told that 'the responsibility which our education service bears for this state of affairs cannot be ignored'.

Certainly the picture has changed little during my teaching lifetime. The issues may be more aggressively articulated. The tune remains the same. As the education lobby pushes for greater recognition and resources, an ever more sceptical public demand that increased expenditure be reflected in such things as improved academic standards and a greater sense of responsibility in young people.

To an extent educationalists have fallen into a pit of their own making. Schools *are* important but schooling, of itself, is not going to reshape society, transform industry, reduce crime or make football supporters behave like devout pilgrims visiting a holy shrine.

Children spend some five and a half hours a day in a classroom for 40 weeks a year. The mathematics of this are worth contemplating – 27½ hours a week, 1100 hours in 365 days, about one eighth of a calendar year. If we relate these figures to others, for example the recent finding that young children spend 25 hours per week watching television (1300 hours per 365 days) we realise that, while schooling may provide a significant element in a child's formative years, it is by no means the only or most pervasive one – nor is it, for many children, necessarily the most important.

When I started teaching the assumption which underpinned most primary schools was that schools were exclusive places. They excluded parents, often on the grounds that teachers knew best. The 1950s were characterised by a division between home and school. Parents were invited into the school on certain days (like the annual open day, prize day, the school play and the Christmas service). On these occasions the children, suitably primed, could be paraded before their admiring parents. There were, of course, Parent-Teacher Associations but these were often merely a useful means of formalising the relationship between home and shcool. When a child, perhaps under pressure for some misdemeanor, observed that 'Mum will be up to school about this', the threat was a real one. Confrontation, when it came, was often tense and sometimes violent. Parent and child were on one side of a chasm called school, the teacher on the other.

The divide was confirmed in all manner of ways. Visitors, particularly parents, were not welcomed in school. A notice by the door, printed by the local authority, often confirmed the point. Parents clustered around the gates at the beginning and end of the school day. Inside the playground, close to the gate, a line was painted. It marked an invisible wall over which only the bravest of parents would venture.

Fortunately, attitudes slowly changed. Teachers and parents have come to realise that the education of children is a joint responsibility, particularly as children are at school for such a small proportion of their waking lives. To help their children benefit from schooling, parents need to understand what happens in school, to appreciate that methods of teaching have changed in the 15 or 20 years since they were themselves pupils in an infant or junior classroom.

The involvement of parents to the extent which now obtains in the majority of our primary schools comes as something of a shock to teachers visiting English primary schools from overseas. It has happened in an ad-hoc way, growing out of need and not out of legislation, or as a consequence of dictates from local or central government.

The roots of parental involvement go back to the 1950s when primary schools began to have an identity of their own, an identity far removed from the old all-age elementary schools of pre-war years. The growing fashion for child-centred education demanded that classrooms became learning centres rather than lecture theatres. Classrooms became ever more informal and when new schools were built their very shape and design proclaimed acceptance of a way of thinking about young children's learning which was often quite alien to the more traditional views of parents. Working in such a school in the mid-1950s, part of my task as a very inexperienced junior teacher was to explain almost daily to parents that Peter or John or Mary *would* learn their tables, *and* learn to compute, despite the fact that they were using apparatus rather than sum books and were active rather than passive.

A second strand which contributed to change was the media. Parents (and much of my work was in the poorer areas of the inner city) were better informed. Television, radio and even the popular press carried regular snippets of educational material. The educational establishment, wishing to promote their service, was not slow in fuelling this new interest.

Further impetus to parent teacher co-operation was given by the Plowden Report (1967) which devoted a whole chapter to 'Participation by parents'. Stressing the fact that home and school are in a state of continuous interaction, the report emphasised the importance of parental attitude.

A strengthening of parental encouragement may produce a better performance in school and this may stimulate the parents to encourage more: discouragement at home may initiate a vicious downward slide.

Examples were used in the report to indicate the approaches to enlist the help of parents which had been adopted in some schools. It is interesting to summarise them here, for instead of being the exceptions that once they were, they are now commonplace:

- Helping children to adapt to school life by adopting a sensitive admissions policy. Parents can be just as sensitive to school as their five-year-old child.
- Encouraging parents to attend school assembly on a regular basis.
- Regarding the parent body as a potential task force – using the technical skills of parents within school to improve the school fabric and the school grounds.

- Improving the communication system between school and home so that *all* parents have the opportunity to develop a positive image of their child's school.
- Using the parent body as a means of raising additional finance.
- Establishing Parent Teacher Associations, Parent Associations, Friends of the School groups.
- Encouraging dialogue between individual parent and individual teacher so that each child can be given specific help and encouragement, discussion between parent and teacher being seen as a better way of evaluating progress than a written report.

While the Plowden Report was influential in giving approval to an expansion of home-school links, it was to some extent reflecting the social climate of the times.

In 1961 the National Pre-School Playgroup Association was formed. This initiative owes much to Belle Tutaev who, while pioneering for an expansion of state-financed nursery education, suggested that mothers might like to establish their own 'playgroups'. The idea met with a widespread response. In the early years the playgroup movement flourished in middle class areas where parents had the skills necessary to establish, fund, organise and supervise a group. Today, with support from charities (like 'Save the Children') and local education authorities (who have provided training courses for playgroup leaders) the movement has expanded. Currently there are some 14 000 playgroups serving nearly 250 000 children.

The playgroups, at first regarded with some suspicion by teachers since they depended upon a mixture of untrained staff and volunteers, have now become an established part of the educational scene. They have provided valuable pre-school experience for children and helped many parents to understand that schools are not the only places in which young children learn.

The 1970s and 1980s have been marked by an ever increasing realisation of the importance of home–school relationships. Many of the practices identified by Plowden have been formalised. The Education Act of 1981 required that each school prepare a document which set out for parents its aims, objectives, organisation and curriculum policy. Parents are now represented on the governing bodies of schools (see Chapter 9). The annual report which head teachers make to the school's governing body is now (as a consequence of the provisions of the 1986 Education Act) presented to parents for discussion at an open meeting; school records are available for inspection. Indeed the climate has changed so radically and rapidly that some teachers feel over-exposed to parental demand, exploitation and expectation.

Such a viewpoint, though no doubt sincerely held, is unfortunate. Young children are shaped as much in the home as they are outside it. Teachers cannot expect to foster a child's all-round development if the child's roots are ignored. For example, how many teachers knew, before Plowden highlighted the fact, that in 1967, 29% of homes in England and Wales possessed five books or less? If a third of the adult population viewed reading with so little enthusiasm, was it any wonder that many children were doubtful as to its worth?

Formalisation of relationships between home and school was a main plank of the education policy of the Thatcher administrations of 1979 and 1983. The aim of this policy was to define parental rights and incidentally, mobilise parents by giving them more influence within the schools their children attended. Some local authorities also encouraged parental involvement, by setting up consultative panels of parents. In ILEA, for example, representatives of the parents of all schools in a division meet regularly to debate matters of mutual concern.

However one views these initiatives (whether they stem from local or central government) they are covertly political – to ensure that schools broadly reflect parental wishes (for parents, being instinctively conservative in matters educational, provide the most effective brake on radical local initiative) or to give public credibility to the educational programme of a particular local authority ('We, the elected councillors, have discussed this with parents and . . .')

The tightening control of schools by politicians (of right, left and centre) was made easier to achieve because teachers and parents had made schools more open, more community conscious. Parents (who were also electors) *were* in schools, helping teachers, involving themselves in school based reading projects like PACT.[2] In many schools there are PTAs and School Associations which, though not political (in a party sense), have shown themselves willing to confront the local authority – be that 'authority' an individual headteacher, a school staff or the divisional or county education officer – when moved to do so.

Parental demands are particularly felt in middle class areas. Possessed, as middle class parents are, of the necessary social and political skills, they can bring considerable pressure to bear upon the schools which their children attend. When pressure is successful the values and aspirations reflected in the school are often those of the parents.

In areas of economic and social deprivation, such 'parent lobbies' are invariably less in evidence. The difficulty experienced by many who teach in these areas is not in keeping parents out of school but in attempting to make them feel that they have a place within it.

Cynically one might observe that the articulate have seized the opportunity to use schools more politically than ever before, disadvantaging still further the already disadvantaged.

The way in which schools are funded in England and Wales tends to compound this division. The school which, for whatever reason, enjoys parental support, is able to use parents as a means of increasing its resources. The resource might be labour (mother sewing curtains frees the infant helper to do something else). The resource might be a skill given freely for which the school might otherwise have to pay (a father digging a pond, laying a path; a mother erecting a simple weather station). Often the resource is money, which allows the school staff to develop the curriculum in ways which would be impossible where capitation from the local authority is the only source of income.

Looking back over some lectures I gave in the early 1980s, I note that the division between the schools which could raise money and those which could not was even then causing me concern. I note that in the academic year 1979–80 the parents in the school in which I then worked provided voluntary donations of £878. To this a further £1425 was added from charities. £4725 was contributed by parents to meet the cost of extended visits to coast and countryside and £1260 was raised to help meet the incidental costs for extra curricula activities. In addition to this, parents were charged for school photographs (£144) and for books purchased through the school book club (£540). Thus, in 1979–80 a primary school of 210 children from 113 families raised £8970 over and above its capitation – an expenditure per child from non public funds of £42.71 per year (£1 per child per school week).

These figures, which are not untypical, underline a school's dependence upon parental and non-state support. The school from which these figures are taken enjoyed excellent financial support from the local authority. It was therefore fortunate both in the capitation it received and the extra financial support provided by an active and caring parent body.[3]

This dependence upon parental support, though necessary if schools are to survive, is socially divisive. There are many schools, particularly in inner cities, where such support will never be forthcoming. Spare money does not exist. Once again the disadvantaged have their disadvantage confirmed.

We would do well to take heed of the American experience. In the United States parents are actively encouraged to play a full and responsible part in their school and their school district. This is commendable in districts where parents have a contribution to make. Nevertheless, by selective choice, the articulate, financially secure and politically active can also indirectly contribute to school failure – not perhaps in their district and their child's school, but in the schools and districts to which such influence is never brought (or the area from which they have moved away).

Until comparatively recently, primary schools, being intimate communities, were places where children, parents and teachers came together and where common sense and common purpose stilled the strident demands of the politically extreme.

Now it seems that the goodwill that once existed has been largely destroyed. The teaching force, disillusioned and aggrieved at the treatment it has received from a succession of Secretaries of State, has been less willing in recent years to devote unpaid hours to community bridge-building. Parents, surprised at the effects which a deliberate withdrawal of voluntary labour brought in its wake, have become angered and disenchanted.

Opportunism is the mark of the successful politican. With teachers' morale at its lowest ebb in living memory and with parental frustration escalating, the way was clear for Central Government to demand that schools be made much more accountable – accountable to the parent body which the teachers had for years struggled to involve in schools in the interests of the children they were teaching.

With slick efficiency successive Conservative administrations have used teacher unrest (for which they must take a considerable share of responsibility) as a justification for taking an even firmer control of the whole education service. To further this end the idea of parent power has been encouraged, giving legal formality to the hitherto informal partnership of teacher and parent.

Only time will tell whether such a plan will create the schools our children deserve. As many a parent on the mainland of Europe could observe, legislation cannot force co-operation, neither can it create harmony in school. If, as I have discovered from studying continental educational systems at first hand, fixed contracts bring fixed commitments, our children (and their parents) will be the poorer for it.

Notes and references

1 More recent research suggests that 'will' rather than 'may' should have been used to condition the verbs in this sentence.
2 PACT: Parents And Children and Teachers. In schools where PACT is followed, the reading progress of each child is jointly monitored at home and at school. Parents are helped to appreciate how children come to master reading. They undertake to listen to their child read on a regular basis and to keep in constant touch with the teacher.
3 Nationally, the sum raised for schools by parents within the state sector rose by 170% in the period 1979–86.

9 School into community/ community into school

It is difficult to describe the typical English primary school. As we have seen in earlier chapters, some local authorities prefer to organise their schools within a 5–11 pattern (each school containing the full primary range), in others an infant (5–7)–junior (7–11) pattern is followed. A minority of local education authorities favour a first (5–8/9) and middle school (8/9–12/13) structure. Whatever the pattern adopted, every Authority contains a number of church schools (Church of England, Roman Catholic, Jewish and interdenominational), serving to remind us that in England and Wales schools have local roots.

Despite this parochial focus, schools have continuously been subject to the intervention of central government and a succession of Acts of Parliament since 1870 has shaped the pattern, content and organisation of school life. The system, unlike many of its European counterparts, has never been enshrined within one all-embracing piece of parliamentary legislation. In effect the English system depends (for success or failure) upon a range of checks and balances.

The responsibility for ensuring that education is provided for all children according to their 'age, needs, aptitudes and abilities' is vested in the Minister (the Secretary of State for Education) and his department. The task of organising the schools is devolved upon the local education authorities who, in turn, expect headteachers to organise the schools so that the policies which the local authority favours (eg transfer at 11) are implemented.

The headteacher therefore holds a key role in the education chain, interpreting local and national objectives so that they are appropriate to the children for whom he/she is responsible. This responsibility has been defined as follows:

> The headteacher shall control the conduct and curriculum, the internal organisation, management and discipline of the school, the choice of equipment, books and other resources, methods of teaching and the general arrangement of teaching groups and shall exercise supervision over teaching and non teaching.

The headteacher is not as all-powerful as this definition seems to imply, for responsibility for 'curriculum and conduct' also falls within the province of the school governors.

Each school has its own Board of Governors. The contribution which governors could make to the running of a school was examined by the Taylor Committee (which reported in 1977). Essentially governors (formally called 'Managers') represent the 'lay public' and fulfill a watching brief over each local school. When I began my teaching career the chairman of the school managers was a shadowy figure seen on school prize day or when the local authority needed to be encouraged to hasten emergency repairs to the school building. In those days, school managers were little more than extensions of the local political parties, for the position was almost invariably granted to party stalwarts as a reward for years of canvassing or for addressing envelopes during election campaigns. Sometimes this method of 'selecting' managing bodies brought valuable insights into school. More often it meant that party politics divided managers at their termly meetings as keenly as it did on the hustings.

The 1981 and 1986 Education Acts[1] strengthened the power of the school governors considerably, stressing the need for the governing body to examine, in much more detail than had applied before, the 'curriculum and conduct' of the school for which it was responsible. School policy remained the responsibility of the headteacher and staff, but such policy could now be questioned, examined and evaluated.

Following upon the Taylor Report, the governing bodies themselves underwent change. Appointment to the old boards had been within the gift of local power groups (invariably reflecting political affiliations). Political appointments continued to be made (though in reduced numbers) and to each board came elected representatives of teachers, parents and ancillary staff. The aim was to make each governing body more truly representative of the schools they served. The appointment of parents to serve as governors aimed at making the school more accountable to the parent body and by giving parents access to hitherto confidential material, a more responsible voice in the running of the school that their children attend.

This sharing of power has, with but few exceptions, been successfully implemented. Parents, through their elected representatives, can now feel that they have some part to play in the appointment of the headteacher and senior staff.[2] Complaints, observations, suggestions from the parent body can be routed directly to the governors. But parent governors are more than watchdogs, and to view them only in this way is to diminish their role. Parent governors can and do help reduce tension between teaching staff and parent body, they can and do explain the more incomprehensible workings of the local authority to fellow parents. 'I know what the headteacher is saying to you is accurate. I was at the meeting at divisional office with her'.

The expanded role of governors is an indication of a changing political climate (see page 35). Schools must be seen to be more accountable to the community they are there to serve. To 'govern' a school effectively, however, requires a modicum of training. Elected governors expect to have a role, a reason for being elected. To serve a school each governor will need to learn how the education service works; how, for example, special needs children are assessed, how children are transferred between schools, how staff are appointed, the rights of parents should their son or daughter be suspended. In addition to these factual matters they will need to develop a number of important skills. How should an application form for a teaching position be interpreted? What contributes to a successful interviewing technique? How do I ensure that local authority policies (on, for example, equal opportunities) *are* being implemented in the school to which I have been appointed? If such policies are being ignored, what can I do to reawaken awareness of them?

The early 1980s will be seen to have been years of educational change. Many of the changes wll be no more than cosmetic unless funds are made available to implement them. The new breed of school governor needs training and training will consume resources. It is one aspect of educational change which successive Governments have refused to face. Policies on paper can look impressive. They are worthless if they cannot be implemented.

The greater responsibility given to governors is an indication of a desire to make schools more responsible to community hopes and aspirations. Such a policy brings with it some dangers. Elected parent governors may seek to use meetings to confirm local fears and prejudices. Schools tend to see their work against a longer perspective than even the best intentioned parent, the most worthy political appointee.

In many areas the primary school of the 1980s has also been struggling to meet another pressure – the demand that the curriculum which children follow take into account the multicultural nature of contemporary society.

Schools, it is argued, have for too long reflected the values of the white middle class. The curriculum, with the respect it shows for all things Anglo Saxon, makes little acknowledgement of the many children whose background is neither white, middle class nor Christian, nor whose mother tongue is English.[3]

The demand for change which such cultural diversity brings

has not yet touched many of the English shires. It is something to which all schools must sooner or later address themselves. Children now growing up in the Yorkshire Dales or along the Devon coast will find themselves as adults in a nation whose culture has been enriched by its most recent wave of immigrants. We, the indigenous population, may resent the more extreme demands made by activists representing minority groups, but the intensity of the feelings they express is surely a comment on how effective has been their exclusion from the mainstream of life, economic and political. The demand, for example, for Muslim schools to receive financial support from the state, is not unreasonable when we remember that the schools of Christians and Jews are largely state funded.

By continuing to support the exclusive character of a proportion of our schools, we foster unnecessary divisions in society. Perhaps in the not-too-distant future, denominational schools will be seen to be the historical anachronism that they are. We must remember that the great majority of today's schools *are* secular. Although all schools (under the provision of the 1944 Act) are expected to begin the day with a corporate 'act of worship' this requirement is as often ignored as it is honoured.

Secular schools do not necessarily mean that the traditional values of our society must be undermined and swept away. Rather, they mean that the children of all faiths and of none are able to grow together. In doing so, children undoubtedly come into contact with views at variance with those held at home. Religious schools may well enable children to grow up with a particular identity. They also serve to set them apart from the wider community in which they will eventually live and work.

The debate on how our schools can draw strength from cultural diversity as easily as they have done from cultural singularity will continue for years to come. Many primary schools have already made tentative first steps to meet the challenge and richness which multiculturalism brings. Where this has been successful, teachers have looked first at the community beyond the school gates. What do the children from this community need of us? What are their parents' perceptions of school and schooling? What can these children bring into school which will vivify and give point to their learning? What areas of the curriculum do we need to rethink in order to make learning relevant for these children? A French-speaking child of eight could perhaps be introduced to the wonders of Norman architecture and the death of King Harold. It is much more difficult to justify such a study if the class is composed of children whose mother tongues are Bengali, Gujarati, Urdu, Twi and Fanti.

The community which schools serve is not the area beyond the school gates, stretching in every direction that the eye can see. Rather it is the community of people with whom the school identifies and who in turn identify with the school. These would include parents, grandparents, pre-school children and their parents, the community policeman, the street crossing lady, the local authority librarian, the school nurse and doctor, the local rabbi, priest, youth leader, children who have left the school to pass on to secondary education and, of course, the pupils themselves.

There is a sound reason for this viewpoint. Because we are human we are more likely to succeed in any social venture when we stress its human dimension. We cannot hope to see or act within the concrete wastelands of our inner cities. But we *can* act upon and work through the people who live within them.

In this sense accountability implies rather more than a school achieving a broadly acceptable standard in traditional subject areas like mathematics, English or environmental studies. The learning programme which a school adopts must *take into account* and build upon the traditions and aspirations which are articulated by its community – be these traditions Afro-Carribean, Asian, or Anglo-Saxon.

The majority of the educational initiatives of recent years (be they national, local or school based) have stemmed from the realisation that schools need to be made responsible to the expectations of parents, the needs of children and to the broader demands of society. In the process of achieving this end, perceptions of schooling have sharpened.

Education is a continuous process. From birth to death we learn. Schools can escalate the process of understanding, but if schooling is to be effective it should not be seen as a series of isolated and unrelated blocks. The child does not change as he/she moves from school to school. John at five may be smaller than he will be when he reaches the age of 12, but he is the same child. Diversity of approach has been the strength of English primary education. It has also been its weakness.

While acknowledging that diversity can (and often does) bring richness, some educationalists would suggest that such diversity of approach brings with it dangers, not the least of which are repetition of experience and too broad a curriculum focus. In the light of such criticism, the need to maintain an individual approach to young children's learning and at the same time give continuity and coherence to school life has become an overriding concern. The answer may seem to be in the adoption of tightly conceived curriculum guidelines. If so, I think it would be the wrong one.

There is ample evidence, both in England and from abroad, that when tight goals are laid down against which each child's academic progress is measured, teachers tend to teach *to* the objectives rather than to take children beyond them. Even in Croydon (SE London) where a broad curriculum guideline has been presented in the form of a discussion document to teachers and parents, the difficulties of designing a curriculum which will be appropriate to all children are widely acknowledged. The problem does not arise from curriculum design but from the nature of children.

A child can only move forward intellectually from the point he/she has currently reached. The curriculum cannot begin from a base which assumes that every child enters school at the same development stage or that progress through each subsequent stage will be even and untroubled.

The problems which can arise when such an assumption is

made are currently troubling many Swedish teachers. Working to a state *läroplan* (curriculum) which lays down curriculum areas (and the hours and minutes which are to be devoted to them through each school year) acts as a brake upon the majority of children. What do you do as a teacher when the läroplan tells you to teach reading and writing to seven year olds[4] when the seven year olds, new to school, can already read and write?

But to return to the Croydon initiative. Even in this document 'should' is more in evidence than 'must' or 'will', the phrase 'most children' is preferred to 'all children'. Such caveats abound. Although it is perhaps unfair to point to a particular curriculum area to highlight the difficulty inherent in achieving a balanced approach to schooling, forgive me if I do so. According to the Croydon guidelines, children will be encouraged to develop practical skills. One of the skills listed is 'singing in tune'. In my experience some children (and adults) can and do, a minority never will. Again I learn that children will be 'encouraged to perform in time with a good sense of rhythm'. These are innate gifts whose development can be encouraged in school. They cannot be taught. As a cathedral chorister I had no difficulty in singing in tune. As one who has come to the clarinet late in life my music teacher would even now confirm my singular inability to master time and rhythm.

Making teachers accountable by imposing upon them external yardsticks may give some superficial continuity to school life. It will not, of itself, make learning coherent. Each individual interprets experience in his or her own way. Coherence, the shaping of learning and the interpretation of it, cannot be imposed, for it is fashioned within each individual child.

What is needed now – more than ever before – is for teachers to meet and talk. The insularity which has grown from the artificial divisions labelled Nursery, Infant, Junior, Secondary, need to be pulled down. There are too few in-service courses which unite teachers, too many which divide, divisions which are reflected in the trade union organisations which teachers join.

As we have seen in Chapter 8, this sharpening perception of education has encouraged discussion on who should bear the responsibility for schools and schooling. Should not more checks be built into the system to prevent another Tyndale? The strengthening of the role of the Governors, accompanied by the publication of each school's annual report will undoubtedly strengthen the hand of parents and make school staffs much more accountable.

In some local authority areas each annual report now includes an element of forward planning, each school being required to indicate curriculum areas which are to receive particular attention in the future academic year. Where specific local authority initiatives have been demanded (eg on race, sex and class) progress on their implementation is also monitored through the annual report.

All of these measures suggest that the dialogue between school and home is being formalised and that the voice of the parent is now to be both heard and acted upon. New provisions within teachers' contracts give parents an additional right, that of regular interviews with their child's teachers.

No doubt all of the more radical approaches to bring together school and home will strengthen the influence of the parent. My experience of working in areas of affluence and areas of poverty would suggest that the measures which have been adopted will not produce the results their designers intend. The semi-literate parent, broken by poverty, poor housing and unemployment may sincerely wish to express a viewpoint about school and schooling. The first generation immigrant, struggling to master a second language, may have a viewpoint too. Parents like these are unlikely to be able to respond to documents which require facility with words, or to have the ability to articulate demands.

Set these parents – who in some schools make up the majority of the parent body – against those in more prosperous districts. The response to a school's report or its future plans could be destructive as well as supportive.

Parents do have a right to play a full part in their child's education, to give advice, to make suggestions, to criticise. As a headteacher, however, in a school which was always open to parents, my role was often to protect children from the unreasonable demands made upon them by parents whose single purpose seemed to be to bask in the academic success of their offspring.[5] I also spent much time correcting the view that education, to be effective, needs to be identical to that experienced by parents when they were children. This viewpoint is commonly found wherever one teaches. It was touched upon in Plowden. 'People tend to accept what they know and do not demand things they have not experienced'.

The danger, as I see it, is that educational progress may be slowed down and even halted if the initiatives of individual teachers and particular schools are blocked by parental intervention.[6] The history of English education is sprinkled with the names of individual teachers and individual schools who have pioneered a way for others to follow. The contribution may have been in the field of school organisation and management or in approaches to particular subject area.

Change and innovation almost invariably causes anxiety for some parents. Children, they argue, have but one chance to move through primary schooling; it is too precious to be squandered on experiment.

This proposition is weakened when it is realised that the great majority of teachers are also traditionalists. Teachers do not seek to make changes in order to disenfranchise children. Changes in school curriculum, policy and organisation are just as threatening to teachers as they are to parents. It's so much easier to offer the same type of school day, year after academic year. Developments in music, drama, the arts, creative writing, acceptance by teachers that to make progress in mathematics and science the conceptual growth of children needed to be understood (rather than, as it had largely been, ignored) sprang from the thoughtful observation of individual children in classrooms across the country. Perceptive teachers shared their observations – at seminars, at local teachers' centres, college and university – with their colleagues, and with the local and national inspectorate. Indeed it might be argued that in admitting the need for change teachers were acknowledging that their previous practice had not been as effective as it might have been.

Such a standpoint must be seen against the catastrophy of a Tyndale. Teachers, parents and the society of which both are part share the responsibility for providing secure and effective primary schools.

When a school falters it is not always the fault of the teachers or necessarily a comment upon the methods they employ. Neither should failure and low expectations be blamed upon feckless, uncaring parents or demanding, articulate ones. The successful school is invariably one in which parents and teachers are in harmony, disagreements being ones of degree rather than of principle. Schools also depend upon the sensitive support given by the officers of the local education authority and the politicians that they serve, whose decisions will affect the day-to-day running of the education service.

Responsibility for the education of the nation's children cannot be borne by one group of workers – the teachers. It is something which all share. Accountability is indivisible.

Notes and references

1 Circular 681, the 1982 directive from the Department of Education and Science, required for the first time that all curriculum changes made by teaching staff be referred to the school's Governing Body for approval.
2 All of which are appointed to the school through interview (in the first instance when heads are appointed) by the School Governors. The local education authority retains the right of veto.
3 In 1981, of the 3590 children in primary schools in the London Borough of Tower Hamlets (ILEA), 27.6% spoke a mother

tongue which was other than English. For 50 000 children in London schools in 1983, English was the second language. The survey from which these figures have been extracted also noted that 147 different languages were to be found in ILEA schools.

4 In Sweden, compulsory schooling begins when a child has reached the age of 7.

5 How does one respond as a headteacher when a parent enquires whether John (aged 5, having been in school three weeks) will 'obtain at least 6 'O' levels or pass Common Entrance to Winchester at 13'?

6 In 1986 one infant headteacher in Surrey was forced to leave her school as a direct consequence of parent power following disagreements over internal school policy.

10 Contemporary concerns

This book consists of a series of continually recurring themes.
Each theme (be it curriculum or finance, management or
accountability) when examined in any detail, reveals something
of the tensions which touch every primary school in the
country. Should we continue to organise schools on a local,
almost parochial, basis? Should teachers plan the curriculum
or only be given responsibility for organising their daily
programme against a clearly defined national plan? Who
should be responsible for the way a school spends its resources
– the local authority or individual headteachers and their
governing bodies? Are schools to be regarded as agents of
social change forcing children (and their parents) to focus
upon issues such as sexism and racism or should such
initiatives find no place in the classroom? Should the learning
programme which primary children adopt be child centred or
knowledge based? If a knowledge based approach is adopted
will this foster the development of skills and concepts? Is
primary education simply a small unit in a broader educational
scheme or a stage of education in its own right?

Although we may isolate these tensions in order to analyse
them more clearly, in effect they are inter-related. A school
staff which follows a child-centred approach is stating, by
doing so, a view of children and of curriculum design. A
policy statement which articulates views on race, sex and class
is indicating, however obliquely, that the purpose of schooling

is to develop social attitudes as well as to inculcate knowledge.

To disentangle and isolate these interwoven and sometimes conflicting strands is virtually impossible, for they will vary from community to community and the particular significance of any one element will change over time. In periods of consensus (for example in the 1950s when resources were available and education was widely regarded as a means to unify and improve society) tensions are less evident. When consensus is eroded (for example when politics become polarised around radical extremes as they have in the 1980s) then the tensions are much more clearly exposed and identifiable.

The changing points of emphasis in the educational debate can be seen as responses from the education service to developments within the mainstream of society. The educational programme we adopt provides a commentary upon much broader political issues. Thus if the demand for resources exceeds the resources available, the needs of the education service are weighed (nationally and locally) against the demands made by other services. Let me illustrate this with an example.

The Labour administrations of the mid-1970s who sought to control inflation by imposing tighter fiscal controls forced many local authorities to adopt corporate management. When this happened the effect was to run all local services through a Chief Executive and a committee of senior officers. This placed education on the same administrative level as transport, drains, public amenities and town and country planning. The issue facing officers and councillors in this wider forum was not to ask how we shape and fashion educational expenditure but whether it was more socially responsible (and electorally advantageous) to subsidise the village bus services or to spend money on nursery places for the under fives.

Such decisions were taken within a political context, a context far broader than that of education. There was also a knock-on effect. Centralisation of decision making at local government level meant that decisions tended to be made along party lines. As one party caucus fashioned and shaped a policy and managed its implementation through corporate planning, the opposition, itself a party caucus, fought to amend it. When this happened, educational issues (Grammar Schools or Comprehensives, a reduction of nursery school places or higher fees for adults at evening institutes) all too often became party issues and sensitive compromise became less likely.

Fortunately compromise is still to be found in our educational system, being restored when it seems that failure to do so might have unforeseen political consequences. An example of this has been the political response (from all of the major parties) to the small school movement.

In the late 1970s and early '80s village schools were being closed at the rate of one a week. The grounds advanced for closure (whichever political party controlled the local administration) were invariably economic. The argument ran like this: schools with less than 3 teachers were expensive to run. By combining small schools into larger units a broader curriculum could be offered. Moreover children would benefit from the resources and expertise which a larger school could provide – an extensive library, more scientific and technical equipment, a staff with a wider range of skills and experience.

These undoubted economic benefits have to be set against the contribution which small schools make to the life of the community. Supporters of the small school have been vociferous in its defence. 'Close the village school and the village dies with it.' (a cry which is echoed when the church wishes to appoint a rector to run more than one parish or the Post Office decides to close a sub-office).

Political response has been 'considered'. At a time when centralism (both at national and local level) has dominated political thinking and when spending on education has been tightly controlled, small schools continue to survive. One reason, of course, is that English primary education has been built upon small units. Small children *do* need small communities in which to grow and develop. Indeed the size of English

schools, 'domestic' by European standards, invariably evokes
praise from teachers and educational administrators from
overseas.

On the surface, the announcement (in May 1987) by the
Secretary of State that financial considerations would not be
the prime reason for closing small schools appears to be an
acknowledgement that children's needs must, wherever possible, outweigh economic theory, and that localism still has a
contribution to make in a society which is becoming ever more
centrally controlled.

Such a view is naive. Already some analysis has taken place
to determine whether village schools (and schools in depopu-
lated inner city areas) can be kept open as class units rather
than as schools. By appointing a peripatetic head to oversee a
cluster of class units, contemporary economic orthodoxy (and
the centralism which he/she would represent) can be applied
to the education service. At the same time local needs can
appear to be met. Nevertheless this approach, if implemented,
would fundamentally alter the nature of headship. The
headteacher of a 'cluster school' might be in a particular unit
for one day a week (which is hardly likely to be reassuring to
parents).

There would be one other interesting side effect. This
organisational approach, if adopted, would close down a
valuable training ground for teachers. Many successful headteachers have learned their organisational skills by being given
the opportunity to run a small school before being invited to
be responsible for a larger and more demanding one. If cluster
schools develop then this opportunity will be denied and the
headteacher rooted in the local community will become in
many areas little more than a memory. His replacement, an
educational pedlar employed by a remote educational bureaucracy has, for me, very little appeal.

It is clear, therefore, that 'the climate of the times'
(political, economic, social) though difficult to define, shapes
and influences educational policy far more deftly and fundamentally than the wisest local administrator or the most gifted

minister ever could do. The period following the war saw the education service develop with enthusiasm and confidence – so much so that the Plowden Report could recommend that society should positively discriminate in favour of the disadvantaged, a recommendation which was accepted without demur. This surely was confirmation of that liberal tradition which had for so long underpinned English education. To support each child according to his/her individual need (even if this involved unequal distribution of resources) was to acknowledge the right of each child to flower.

How far we have moved from this view! According to one document prepared recently within the Department of Education, this liberal approach has been replaced by stark utilitarianism. In the mid 1980s it would appear that there are inherent dangers in educating chldren to their full potential. 'If we have a highly educated and idle population, we may possibly anticipate more social conflict. People must be educated once more to know their place.'[1] If this viewpoint is widely held then education is no longer about the all-round development of each young citizen but about the exercise of power – political and economic – and is a sad comment on the needs of our future workforce.

Today's primary schools and our understanding of them must, therefore, be seen against the broad sweep of political life. Once this is grasped it is possible to examine the present trends, for these trends, though little more than straws in the wind, will indicate the possible direction that future developments may take.

The curriculum

The debate around the curriculum is central to all change, for he who controls the curriculum controls the school.[2] The arguments for and against a core curriculum have been discussed throughout this book and require little further clarification here. Nevertheless it is worth pondering the grounds which are being advanced for such a policy.

Kenneth Baker, Secretary of State for Education in Margaret Thatcher's second administration, suggested (in a conference speech in January 1987) that nationally agreed objectives will bring 'clarity to the curriculum'. He continued

> There is considerable doubt about how broad the primary curriculum could and should be . . . There is no broad agreement about the balance of the elements within it or about the objectives of each element.[3]

Whilst stressing the need for explicit goals which all teachers will work towards purposefully and without dissipation of effort, the goals are hard to define, to encapsulate in words. If we take a less specific view (as expressed by a fellow minister in Mr Baker's department), the goals of the 'new' curriculum seem identical to those which were advocated by my lecturers during my student days:–

- To equip children with a broad foundation of knowledge, understanding and skills.
- To promote enterprise, intellectual curiosity and constructive questioning alongside a facility for team work and co-operation.
- To give a proper place to practical skills and the application of knowledge and understanding.

This admirable analysis of curriculum needs, as outlined by Angela Rumbold to a Japanese audience in Tokyo in January 1987, had to satisfy certain pre-conditions, the most significant of which was 'to obtain maximum value for money'.

These two quotations, taken from political colleagues working in the same department, throw into sharp focus the curriculum dilemma. It is a dilemma which transcends party lines. The Labour Party has also been converted to centralism – though I doubt a curriculum could be written by an Education Council composed of representatives of local authorities, teachers' unions, parents and industry (the policy offered to electorate in June 1987).

If the curriculum *is* to be centralised then it will require (as it does in Eastern Europe) cohorts of 'experts' to prepare the guidelines and the textual material which supports them. If the national curriculum is to be shaped around well turned, widely acceptable phrases, then how these phrases are interpreted within individual classrooms will remain with the discretion of the teacher. (Thus the actual current position will change very little. Teachers will simply be asked to acknowledge broad, generally-agreed principles).

If the curriculum consists of 'benchmarks' which have been arbitrarily selected to denote progress, some method will have to be introduced to set each child against them. What will such benchmarks denote? Are they to be content based? If so, is content (learned for a test and then forgotten) a satisfactory criteria upon which to base a curriculum? Could these 'benchmarks' centre upon skills and concepts? Should they be age-related or merely be used to measure the stage a child has reached, the skills he/she has mastered, the concepts grasped. If they are age-related how will this affect how the gifted or less able spend their time at school? Is it possible to design a curriculum which meets such individual and personal needs, particularly when, for young children, the very fact of being at school is adding a whole new dimension to life. In this sense school itself and every moment of the day spent within it *is* the curriculum.

Resolving the problem of how to measure the curriculum for each child continues to bedevil educationalists across the world. The assumption, of course, is that the education of each child, in each school, in each town and village, can be measured against some task or objective centrally set. The Government sets the task, which is interpreted by the local authority, delivered by the teacher, and then measured. This assumes that education (which is about the interaction of human beings at a personal and intimate level) can be run like a mechanised production line. Continuous and regular product analysis is appropriate to Ford and Unilever. It is not appropriate to children who, unlike cars or packets of soap, will respond in a human dimension to the system which is used to shape them. Concern for how to improve the quality of the learning experience is in danger of being lost. We need to concentrate rather more on improving the actual process and rather less on analysing what we might teach and how we could then measure whether 'the teaching' has been 'learned'.

It is altogether too simplistic to assume that we can measure children by testing them at 7, 11, and 14. Tests, by their design and nature, serve to indicate what a child has remembered at the moment of testing. They do not measure continuing growth nor comment upon all those things which are known but not tested. Barry Hines in his evocative story of a young boy's relationship with a goshawk makes the point most effectively.[4] Although this example is drawn from a fictional child, it is a cameo which could be repeated by almost anyone who has ever taught.

Testing at 7 and 11 will inevitably lead to unfortunate comparisons caused by the measuring of one child against another. A nation which failed so many of its children by reliance upon selection at 11 seems to have learned so little from the experience!

For any testing to be meaningful there must also be a common starting point. This is one thing which is lacking in the primary years. How do you mark the achievement of David, (taken into local authority care at birth, having been found in a telephone box in a South London backstreet), and Paul, (the son of a flourishing architect), after two years of infant schooling. At five David could hardly speak – and Paul rarely knew when to stop. At five David lacked parenting and could not hold a pencil. At five Paul could read, count and write simple sentences. At seven these two children were academically years apart . . . but David had learned to speak, share, talk. Were his achievements any less than those of Paul?

Continuous assessment, commonly practised by most teachers, does not seek to compare child with child but each child with him/herself. Continuous assessment has been built into the newly introduced GCSE Examination (for children at 16). It is strange that a formal test (with all the tensions that it brings) should be thought to be more appropriate to measure children at 7 and 11.

Discussions about curriculum reform have tended to revolve around how such reforms could be achieved and this has turned attention away from a number of associated issues. In the 1950s and 1960s the purpose of schooling, even at primary level, was discussed against a child's long term needs. To live fully as an adult man or woman, proclaimed Plowden, one must first live fully as a child. In other words the narrow goals of schooling were seen within a long term perspective.

Our national curriculum, when and if it comes, will need to address itself to this broader viewpoint, a viewpoint which is not seen in terms of projected market forces and the narrow needs of prospective employers. Attitudes to such things as learning, the use of leisure, care and concern for others and social responsibility are laid down and confirmed in the primary years. In terms of the society in which our children will eventually live and work, these qualities will surely prove more vital and of greater worth than rote learning which can be measured and assessed. A move towards some centrally agreed code of practice needs to be set against the experience of many other countries which, having a centralised curriculum, are seeking to free themselves from its worst extravagances. In Japan children are rote taught and tested. So stressful and ineffective is this proving to be that even educational traditionalists are now beginning to emphasise the important place which understanding plays in the mastery of information. In West Germany, ministers are seeking to develop a wider intellectual framework within the primary curriculum. In Greece, where traditional methods prevail, the curriculum is being re-examined for, as a recent Minister of Education observed:

> The curriculum must not be overloaded. The child must learn to think and look for the reason for things. The objective is not the creation of neurotic children who will be walking encyclopedias.

Even in France the value of tight centralism has been questioned – and I quote a minister responsible for schools:

> Our teaching is unreal. It condemns itself to failure because it continues to propose images and myths of a society that is not ours. Once and for all we have to prepare our children for their own world and not for that of our grandparents.

Organisation

Once education (ie what happens in schools) can be encouraged to follow some centrally agreed pattern, it becomes far easier to implement new organisational structures. Several changes have been proposed, some more far reaching than others.

One, which has been largely welcomed by the political right wing, would be to make each school more accountable. One cheap and effective way of doing this is through a system of school vouchers. Each parent would receive an education voucher from central government to 'spend' at a school of his/ her choice. For the receiving school this voucher would be 'cashed' and so become the income which would be necessary to maintain and run the school. A school with a high voucher income could expand, whilst a school with a low voucher income would respond to the market (ie change its educational ways) or die. Parents who so chose could add to their vouchers, spending them if they wished in the private sector. This approach, which has been used in some school districts in the United States and flirted with in England, draws inspiration from the economics of radical conservatism. It would, if implemented, energise the private sector (for which no curriculum guidelines are currently suggested!) and expand an education system which confirmed social differences. Schools for the poor would stand alongside houses for the poor. Parent power, at its most insidious, would become a vehicle of school control within an ever more divided society.

Vouchers can also be seen as an extension of the Assisted Places Scheme which was introduced during the first Thatcher administration. Children of primary school age are invited to sit an examination at 11 and, if successful, 'win' a place in a private school. The place is paid for from public funds, the parent being expected to make some contribution if in a financial position to do so. This measure, which was presented as giving parents additional choice, has allowed Central Government to devote funds to the non public sector.

Every place which an 'assisted' child takes up in a fee paying school of quality fills a space which would have been paid for privately. Presumably the non-assisted children (who would otherwise have taken these places) find a vacancy in schools of a slightly lesser quality. The knock-on effect is therefore to squeeze the less academic children of the well-to-do into the less effective private schools. Thus this simple initiative achieves three ends: privatisation is fostered; competent children are diverted from the mainstream of state secondary education; pressure is brought upon the headteachers and staffs of primary schools to teach to selective tests.

The Assisted Places Scheme is also an indication of the movement towards privatisation. The rationale for this policy is 'parental choice'. For there to be true choice, however, any choice must be open to all. For the financially well endowed, decisions can be made by the family to determine whether children attend private or state schools. Such 'choice', however, is not open to the majority of parents. In other words 'choice' is directly related to ability to pay – which means that the school system continues to confirm social and class differences (even at primary school level).

Another idea which has been advanced is that of the City Technology College. It is envisaged that these colleges, for children aged between 11–18, will be established in areas of inner city deprivation. They will be funded by local industry in addition to a direct grant from central government. The children who will attend them will be drawn from the primary schools in their immediate neighbourhood. The curriculum which these children will follow will seek to emphasise new technology (both theory and practical skills).

The most interesting element of this plan is that such schools will be independent of the local educational authority in whose area they stand. Furthermore every primary child who applies for a place will need to undergo some form of selection to gain entry. If CTCs are introduced their presence will have far reaching effects upon all the schools in their immediate area. County secondary schools are likely to be denied their more able pupils (for parents are likely to choose a school which in addition to receiving additional funding seems to be equipped for the world of micro technology and eventual employment in the 'sunrise' industries of tomorrow). At the same time the feeder primary schools will again be pressured into relating their curriculum to the 11 plus selection process which determines CTC entry.

A third, widely debated, approach aims at giving schools far greater autonomy and self management. Under such a scheme, the local authority (or central government) would fund each state school. The headteacher, through the School Governors, would be responsible for the school's budget which could be spent as he/she decides. The head would therefore pay the teachers (the salary scale being determined by mutual consent) and decide how much of the annual income would be spent on such things as books, repairs, secretarial assistance, cleaning, heating and gardening. By firmly placing the total burden of school upon the head and governors, each school could become autonomous. This suggestion, given guarded welcome by Secondary Head-teachers at their Easter conference in 1987, would considerably extend the administrative role of headteachers in primary schools. Often primary schools run with minimum secretarial support, and any further responsibilities placed upon head-teachers would inevitably mean that additional office staff would be required. And who would organise this staff – the headteacher who was appointed to run a school because he/she had specialist skills in *teaching*!

Each of these schemes has been widely acclaimed and equally widely criticised. They draw their strength from a market place, 'good housekeeping' view of education, supporting the view that the customers (the parents) must henceforth have more influence over the schools their children attend. To this I would add another consideration. By giving parents greater power, the influence of the local education authority is reduced. As local power is reduced, central power can be increased.

Politicisation

Throughout this chapter it has been difficult to avoid taking a political stance. Education in the 1980s has become marked by political extremism from both left and right. City Technology Colleges can be presented as a radical approach to inner city decay: they can also be presented as a means of weakening local autonomy.

It could be argued – and with good reason – that a desire to control education by the political right is an understandable response to the educational initiatives pioneered by the political left. For many left-wing councils, administering as they often have areas of high unemployment, poverty and deprivation, educational and social issues are inextricably intertwined. If, as evidence seems to suggest, schools are failing black youngsters, girls and children from financially insecure homes and ignoring the 'rights' of minority groups, then schools have not only to change in themselves but also to become agents of change. From these changes (it is hoped) a more just society would grow.

When schools, through guidelines and policy statements (locally adopted), are used to sensitise parents to issues of race, class, religion and ethnic identity through the curriculum such a policy is bound to be challenged. Is it the school's task to focus upon moral issues? If it is, can it do so within a society which is uncertain as to where its priorities lie? For example do we *really* think that primary schools should, through their curriculum, explore views on homosexuality and have such explorations justified as follows:

> Heterosexuality is not biologically built into us like hunger – we are not all born heterosexual.. We are all born with a sexuality. That most people express their sexuality heterosexually rather than homosexually is because we are socially conditioned to do so.
>
> *(Labour Party discussion document, Outer London constituency)*

Public response to such pronouncements even in the areas where such beliefs are earnestly and sincerely held, has been critical. In considering how our primary schools will develop over the next decade we need to be aware that the polarisation and radicalism of politics have destroyed consensus. While an education born of consensus may be less exciting to work in, I know, from experience, that consensus produces a climate in which both teaching and learning take place more effectively.

Views on education

All that I have written in this book continually invites you, the reader, to reflect on the education of young children. As Lord Richie Calder observed some years ago in a talk on BBC radio, the years since the war have seen fundamental advances in our understanding of the Universe. We have rocketed, with the help of computer technology, from Atom Age to Space Age. 'We are, in the studies of DNA and molecular biology, in predictable possession of the Secret of Life'.

This advance has not been made without considerable cost. Our social institutions respond so slowly to technological advance for they are ill equipped to cope with the new revolutionary forces which scientific advance brings.

This is the nub of our educational problem. Wherever we are employed in education, whenever, as parents, we think of the future our children will enter, we find ourselves unable to conceive of the nature of the world into which they will move. We struggle to make minor adjustments to our institutions, to our school curriculum, to our policy documents, in the hope that as we do so these flimsy changes and the passing ideals which they contain will provide a passport for our children into their tomorrow. If we believe this passport is of any worth, we delude ourselves and in the process handicap our children.

As we in England struggle for a solution to our educational malaise a policy document from the Department of Education, NW Territories, Canada deserves a mention. It states:

Education is based upon two sets of needs. First are the needs of the individual and second are the needs of society.

At first sight this may seem too simplistic a framework upon which to build the primary schools of tomorrow. But is it? Experience has surely taught us that we need to devote ourselves to education rather than to schooling. The challenge of the 1980s and 90s is not to see how far we can retreat into the past but how to equip children with the skills they will need to survive in a rapidly changing society.

We need now, more than ever before, to put children first, to make their needs paramount. Only then can we hope to produce the flexible people who will be equipped, emotionally and intellectually, to face the change and challenge the next century will bring.

Notes and references

1 *The Guardian* 20.8.85, p 11. The quotation is taken from a DES discussion paper.
2 A view which was regarded with apprehension by a non-conformist minister in 1847. 'State power in religion, State power in

education, State power in education, State power in Inspectors, State power in Whitehall reaching all over England are all, as kindred influences against Liberty, against National Spirit.'

3 *Times Educational Supplement* 16.1.87.
4 Barry Hines *A Kestrel for a Knave*.

Bibliography

Adams, F (1986) *Special Education* Longman
Aries, P (1973) *Centuries of childhood* Penguin
Ashton, P *et al* (1975) *Aims into Practice* Hodder and Stoughton
Ashton, P *et al* (1975) *Aims of Primary Education*: A study of Teachers Opinions, Macmillan
Bennet, N (1976) *Teaching styles & pupil progress* Open Books
Blackie, John (1974) *Changing the Primary School* Macmillan
Blatchford, P *et al* (1982) *The first transition – Home to pre school* National Foundation for Education Research (NFER)
Blyth, W (1984) *Development, experience and curriculum in Primary Education* Croom Helm
Blyth, W (1965) *English Primary Education* Routledge and Kegan Paul
Boydell, Deanne (1978) *The Primary Teacher in action* Open Books
Brown, Mary and Precious, Norman (1968) *The integrated day in the Primary School*, Ward Lock
Caldwell Cook, H (1917) *The Playway* Heinemann (1966 edition)
Cleave, Shirley (1982) *And so to school* NFER
Clegg, A and Megson, B (1968) *Children in distress* Penguin
Davie, Ronald (1982) *From birth to seven* Longman
Dean, Joan (1983) *Organising learning in the Primary School classroom* Croom Helm
Deem, Rosemary (1980) *Schooling for Women's Work* Routledge & Kegan Paul
Dearden, R F (1976) *Problems in Primary Education* Routledge & Kegan Paul
Dowling, M and Dauncey, E (1984) *Teaching 3 to 9 year olds* Ward Lock

Eyken, van der, Willen (1973) *Education, the child & society* Penguin

Eyken, van der, Willen (1974) *The Pre school years* (third edition) Penguin

Eyken, van der, Willen and Turner, Barry (1969) *Adventures in Education* Allen Lane

Fontana, D (ed) (1978) *The Education of the young child* Open Books

Galton, Maurice *et al* (1980) *Inside the Primary classroom* Routlege & Kegan Paul

Haigh, Gerald *et al* (1979) *On our side* Temple Smith

Hegarty, S *et al* (1982) *Educating children with special needs in the ordinary school* NFER

Holt, John (1970) *The underachieving school* Pitman

Holt, John (1970) *How children fail* Penguin

Hopkins, A (1978) *The School Debate* Penguin

Inner London Education Authority (1985) *Improving Primary Schools* ILEA, London

Keddie, N (ed) (1973) *Tinker, Tailor (The myth of Deprivation)* Penguin

Kirby, Norman (1981) *Personal Values in Primary Education*, Harper & Row

Maelure, Stuart (1968) *Education Documents, England & Wales, 1816 to the present day* Methuen, (1979 edition)

Marsh, L (1970) *Alongside the child* A & C Black

Midwinter, E (1972) *Priority Education* Penguin

Pluckrose, Henry (1979) *Children in their Primary Schools* Penguin & Harper Row

Pluckrose, Henry (1975) *Open School, open society* Evans Bros

Pluckrose, Henry and Wilby, Peter (1980) *Education 2000* Temple Smith

Pluckrose, Henry and Wilby, Peter (1979) *The Condition of English Schooling* Penguin

Rae, G and McPhillimy, A (1976) *Learning in the Primary School* Hodder & Stoughton

Rex, John (1978) *Five views of multiracial Britain* Commission for Racial Equality

Richards, C (1982) *New directions in Primary Education* The Falmer Press

Ridgway, Lorna (1976) *The task of the teacher* Ward Lock

Rutter, M (1975) *Helping troubled children* Penguin

Sandström C I (1969) *The Psychology of childhood and adolescence* Penguin (1975 edition)
Schools Council (1983) *Primary Practice* Methuen
Sharpe, Sue (1976) *Just like a girl* Penguin
Stone, M (1981) *The Education of the black child in Britain* Fontana
Tough, J (1977) *The development of meaning* Allen & Unwin
Walker, Stephen (ed) (1983) *Gender, Class & Education* The Falmer Press
Wall, W D (1975) *Constructive education for children* Harrap & UNESCO
Yardley, Alice (1978) *Learning to adjust* Evans Bros

GOVERNMENT PUBLICATIONS, all available through Her Majesty's Stationary Office, London
Report of the Central Advisory Council for Education *Children and their Primary Schools* (The Plowden Report) Volume 1, 1967
A New Partnership for our schools (The Taylor Report) 1977
Special Educational Needs (The Warnock Report) 1978
Primary Education in England, a survey by H M Inspectors of Schools 1978
A View of the curriculum, 1980
The School curriculum, 1981
Education 5–9, 1982
9–13 Middle Schools, 1983
The Curriculum 5–16, 1985
Better Schools, 1985
Better Schools – evaluation & appraisal (conference report) 1986

Index